RED STONE HEART

Scrambling High Uinta Peaks

KEVIN HOLDSWORTH

ISBN# 978-1-941052-46-4 Trade Paper
ISBN# 978-1-941052-48-8 eBook
ISBN# 978-1-941052-50-1 Hardback

Library of Congress Control Number:
2020946237

Photographs by the author, Sean McCandless,
Laura M. McCandless and Jerry White.
Photo of Clarence King:
Library of Congress, American Memory Division

Cover Design: Antelope Design
Cover Photo: Sean McCandless

This is a memoir.
Not everyone remembers events in the same way.
These recolections are exclusively those of the author.

PronghornPress.Org

You must not think of a mountain range as a line of peaks standing on a plain, but as a broad platform many miles wide, from which mountains have been carved by the waters.

You must conceive, too, that this plateau is cut by gulches and canyons in many directions, and that beautiful valleys are scattered about at different altitudes.

—John Wesley Powell, 1869

Table of Contents

Part III

Schistosity
(1990s)
123

Part IV

The Talus Palace
(2000-2005)
183

Part V
Island Wilderness
(2006-2012)
243

RED STONE HEART

Scrambling High Uinta Peaks

Prelude
South Paul Knob
2007

The most difficult conditions for winter travel occur when there is enough snow to make walking difficult or impossible but not enough to provide a smooth cover over which to ski or snowshoe. The rocks stick out far enough to make skiing impossible, the snowshoes take a terrible beating and tend to sink and jam between boulders, and the walker finds himself plunging repeatedly through the unconsolidated snow.

—Raymond Bridge
America's Backpack Book, 1973.

Scrambling High Unita Peaks

Extravagant claims about the alleged ease of Paul Peak, 12,143 feet, coax us into contemplating a trek up Swift Creek in April of a dry year. The claims are based on looking at maps rather than intimate knowledge. You look at a map and think that the lay of the land will be different from what it probably is. Snug in your den, you forget just how far a section of bad conditions can stretch.

Not many people would consider bagging an Uinta peak in April of a dry year to be a good thing to do. There will be snow, and there will not be snow. Still, the high country can be wildly fresh this time of year, before the greening renewal sets in. The land is empty of other distractions, no aspen leaves quaking or new grass rustling, just the sound of wind against rocks and the voices of stream flow.

In Price, Utah, the night before, I give a reading from *Big Wonderful* to a small, friendly crowd, and next morning head over Indian Canyon in the Cherokee, with an exaggerated sense of self-importance, seldom useful, and seldom lasting on a slog. Arriving at the trailhead before the others, I spread out my gear on a picnic table and re-contemplate my choices. The trail to the high country leads up a steep south-facing hill. The promise of the hill is dry. There isn't a lingering tongue of icy whiteness on the whole slope, not a shaded drift of slush. This isn't exactly a surprise. Swift Creek sits on the South Slope of the Uinta Mountains. The South Slope means low starts and high finishes.

Higher up there will be snow. Where and when we reach it is anyone's guess. Getting to the

snow will involve carrying the tools of the trade on our backs. Yet again I debate: skis or snowshoes, snowshoes or skis? Springtime mountaineering in the Rockies is impossible without one or the other. I've brought both. Which to pick has been the email subject for weeks.

Just to be honest, while crossing dry ground I've carried skis, boots and accessories on my back for miles at a time and find little to recommend it. That's twenty pounds just for the privilege. It makes nearly any other sporting activity look good. On the other hand, a pair of snowshoes (webs, flip flops) tip the scale at four pounds and strap neatly onto the sides of a backpack without sticking up like antennae. Better yet, using webs you can wear the same boots the entire trip, particularly if you own some overwrought Italian-leather mountaineering boots, footwear that never gets used much except for trips like these. The only problem with this thinking is that on snow, skis are totally superior.

Still, waiting at the base of the snowless south-facing hill, I'm unable to see any reason why I should carry skis.

I cinch my webs to the pack, look at the tidy little package, and hope I'm making the right decision.

A person wouldn't undertake this kind of trip alone. It's necessary to have co-conspirators, partners in the climb. Mine arrive from Salt Lake near the appointed time: Sean and Larissa McHelen, Tee Trundler and dogs Maggie and Boomer show up in Larissa's Cherokee: three humans, two dogs, and a pile of gear. How they crammed that much in is miraculous. One of the items that Tee and Sean neglected or forgot to bring, though, is their snowshoes. Larissa brought hers but isn't going to break rank. No, they will "ski."

In no hurry, we dawdle around, eat lunch, sort gear, catch up about the winter, the Jazz, and avoid the inevitable hard dry work ahead. There isn't any debate or "you'll be sorry" or claims about whether skis or snowshoes will be better. Who can say? We make our choices and will live with them. The worst is to have neither, but that, fortunately, is another story.

Finally, unable to put it off any longer, up we trudge. The snowless hill soon provides soulful low and highland views. We pass through marvelous little airy clearings that would provide delicious picnic spots for ourselves as eagles. We traipse the crest of an old lateral moraine, right on the knife edge. Steep forest sweeps down on both sides, and we hear the stream far below. Early in the year as it is, we feel the thrill of being the first humans to pass through the land. We follow much bobcat sign. We wonder if the bears are out.

As the trail eventually levels out and the first snow patches appear, we imagine that the way will get easier. Instead, the trail loses elevation and becomes more snow-choked at the same time, snowy but not snowy enough. Horrible. Neither set up works.

Originally, we had intended to try to reach the upper end of the big meadow beneath the slopes of Paul Peak and camp there, a place that now seems too far away to reach. "Originally" is the big talking that takes place at home and not on site. "Originally" doesn't carry a heavy pack with towering antlers.

Worn down by the carrying, disgruntled by the slippery sections of the icy trail, and never having been able to don our tag-a-longs, we decide to stop at the first good water source. We come to a pour-over in a small winter-matted meadow, find a campsite in an adjacent aspen copse with a very old fire ring, set up, kick back, start a fire, and ready ourselves for what will be an early start tomorrow.

Everything is frozen in the early morning chill. We make quick progress, crossing icy tongues of snow, crunching over frozen rivulets, slip-sliding up slopes of grass and willow. The day progresses with a flavorful selection of brambles, aspen groves, a face of bare talus, and a snowy flat in the upper basin. We don't talk much, or if we do, it's just about discomfort. There aren't a lot of helpful things to say.

All the way we carry our skis or snowshoes. Finally, in early afternoon, we reach snowfields that are already showing a lot of rock, red and purple necklaces. Maybe we should have come in March. Maybe we shouldn't have come at all.

We finally put things on our feet. Sean, Larissa and Tee fasten their skis while I cinch my snowshoes.

At last, more customary traveling. We make good time for a couple of miles and reach the top of nondescript South Paul Knob at 11,748 feet. We consider continuing to Paul Peak proper. Although it's close enough (a couple of miles) and look, we have skis, but we wouldn't get up it and all the way down before dark. Not a chance. Descending all the stuff we'd come up isn't going to be a whole lot easier than going up and would be dangerous in the dark.

I know where I'm not going. Paul Peak is not calling, not now anyway. Larissa agrees with me, but thanks them for asking. Sean and Tee talk about it bigly and agree it's not the day for it.

We console ourselves with a birds-eye glimpse of the weirdly wintered upper Swift Creek basin where a dozen lakes lie, ovals, recumbent and white. We study the high lonesome Emmons ridge, talking about how this is the year for it, the Big E. Some solace, too, we find in the knowledge that not many people visit this spot. Why would they?

RED STONE HEART

On the way down the three skiers, Tee, Sean and Larissa and their dogs will be way ahead of me. Even in mushy snow skis are about five times faster. I figure we'll go down the same way we came up, and hopefully they'll wait for me toward the bottom.

Some distance down the ridge, though, they drop into a north-east facing bowl, earning some quick turns for their mammoth uphill effort. I peer over the edge and into the bowl. They're already halfway down, ripping it up.

I notice two things: The first is that the slopes are way too steep for snowshoes. The second is that at the bottom of the bowl there stretches a veritable sea of talus and loose, scattered boulders, something they might have overlooked in their excitement to justify their means. Although it'll probably be possible to stay high and traverse around most of it, the skiers will face some rocky trouble between the snow bowl, the timber and the stream. Also, their orientation is a quarter-compass wedge in the wrong direction. The skiing looks great, though.

They stop halfway down. I holler that I'll be going back the way we'd come and would see them back at camp.

"Be careful."

"You too."

And so, we separate.

Not wanting to see them enjoy their few remaining great and glorious turns, I scamper around the corner, regain our previous route, and begin to feel myself very much alone. In such a situation, you gain a sudden surge of adrenaline. Rather than plunging ahead and wasting energy, I sit down on a rock, have a snack and some water, and begin talking to myself. The deal's pretty simple.

You're alone. Get down. Get back. You have a wife and children. Be safe.

To assuage my concern and fear, I try to visualize each section of the route, break it into manageable pieces. I'm nervous about the talus face and the muddy slopes below. At least I'll be able to get down the steep parts soon. The lowland forest will be easier.

Following the blessed tracks, I flip flop my way down the upper slopes. I cross the flat and notice a frozen lake we'd missed on the way up, snake around some groves of spruce and fir and shy away from moats and melt outs.

I don't want to rest at the top of the crux (the bare, steep, loose talus face) because it just puckers me up. I only want to get down. I can see our morning's tracks tiny at the bottom. The face is longer and looser on the way down. *You've been down much worse stuff before. Pick up your pole, Rambo. Take it easy. You're flailing. Watch the pack. Almost there. Gingerly, carefully.*

At the bottom I notice it had only taken twenty minutes to get down the face, but they were rock-rich rickety minutes. Sweat soaked, I shed a layer.

Another rest before the aspen thrash. I wonder about the others. I feel no anger or sense of betrayal. It makes sense to go our separate ways except that we had separated. Sean will look after Larissa. Larissa will look after Sean. Tee will look after Tee. Will they stay together? Probably not.

Considering it more carefully: Sean is strong but sometimes strongly disoriented and lacks common sense. Larissa is determined as can be, and she'll follow Sean anywhere and has. Tee has plenty of experience but sometimes he likes to take the hard way. He likes a test and to go as Tee-by-Himself.

What if the McHelens get lost? What if they start to disagree? What if they get into trouble? Soon, I no longer want to think about it. "Just worry about yourself," my wife Jennifer would say.

Sometimes it seems a complete wonder that we don't twist ankles or pop out knees in tricky terrain. Perhaps there's an element of being rightly warmed up, like rugby or field hockey players. Maybe it's adrenaline. Maybe it's just dumb luck. But as I slash through the aspen, swinging simian-like from tree to tree and sliding down through soft steep snow and rocks, I wonder. It seems like an easy place to get hurt. *Dohp. You can rest when you get to the timber. Where is the…. Ouch.*

A little fear, a little fatigue, difficult footing and unclear landmarks can disorient a person. This is how people get lost and get hurt. You begin to lose a sense of scale. Why is it taking so long? Where is the darned stream? I can hear it, but it can't really be that far away, can it? Where is the red cliff? You know, that one landmark red cliff? The main trail is on the other side, isn't it? Is it? Bad weather, fatigue, and being alone (or with certain companions) can intensify the effect. Fortunately, the late afternoon weather is fine.

Lower down in the forest travel continues bad and gets worse. The routine devolves to this: put on the webs to walk on snow for a short distance. Hit rocks or dirt. Take off the webs. Walk in the dirt and mud and duff and across the krummholz and manzanita and rivulets and rocks and gravel. Hit more snow. Wallow, friend, wallow. Put on the darned webs or sink, sink, sink. Scoot across the slushy drifts. Hit more rocks, dirt and manzanita. Take 'em off. Go another two-hundred feet. Look for snow. Find snow. Put 'em back on. Go another hundred yards. Take 'em off. Put 'em on. Repeat.

Still, I'm glad again that I don't have skis. It's easy enough to pick up and carry the useless, annoying, garbage-breath, slush-coated, worse-than-anything flip flops. Skis would have been taller, heavier, more exasperating. Walking in plastic tele boots: torture.

It goes on like this for miles, or what seems like miles. I cross many brown, black, green, gray, red and purple places not really meant for snowshoes.

Soon, perhaps I'll be done with the snow, most of it anyway and strap the webs to my pack and will swim, slide and flail down the lingering snowdrifts if I have to. (And I will have to.)

At last, the meadow, the big beaver meadow opens up. Happy moment. I walk its length on hummocks, past old beaver ponds that are beginning to steam up in the shadow, find the trail at the funnel of it, press my boots into the mud as a calling card and sit down to let the strong emotions pass. I'll make it back. It's late in the day now, though, and it sure looks like the others are still back there. How far? How bad is it?

RED STONE HEART

I know if I follow the path, I'll come eventually to the pour-over near camp. I make sure to leave plenty of boot marks in the muddy sections of the trail for the others who follow.

Camp at last. I dump my pack, toss my poles, pull the webs off my pack and fling them to dry, fetch some water, start the stove, pull my boots off, don the camp booties, feel lonely, and then Tee shows up.

Without a word of welcome, he heaves his skis violently into some bushes, uses a crude expletive, tosses his poles in another direction, and uses the crude expletive again. He then hurls his backpack to the ground and pulls off his gloves.

"Hey," I say.

"It's good to see you," he says.

"Yes, good to see you, too."

He'd had a helluva time in the trees, practically a monkey man, he explains. He'd crossed the stream and followed it down, re-crossed it at the beaver meadow. "Man, was I glad to see your boot prints."

"Yeah, I figured you might be behind me. I didn't know. I was sure glad to make them. That was getting kind of long there at the end."

Tee goes back over to his pack, kicks it, kicks his skis, re-tosses his poles, and pulls off his boots. He tells me how long it had been since he'd left the McHelens—a couple of hours, maybe. They'd been doing fine, just slow.

We both know, if it comes to it, that we may have to go out and try to find them or render assistance. The situation does not allow for excessive relaxation.

"Wouldn't want to spend the night out," Tee says.

"No, wouldn't want to be spending the night out just now," I say. "Kinda tired."

"It'll be cold tonight."

"Risky. Cold. Tired."

We'd checked with each other earlier in the day to make sure that everyone had matches, lighter, extra clothes, headlamp...especially matches. It would be impossible not to start a fire in that forest, with so much beetle-killed wood, and so many dry spots to sit on. One cold, crisp way to spend the night: feeding logs to the fire, front warm, back frozen. The night would be long and miserable but entirely survivable.

"They'll show up," he says.

"You know they will." I have to ask, "Hey, how was it carrying those skis in all those trees today?"

Tee looks at me long and seriously. He uses a crude expletive. "Where's the whiskey?"

Hot drinks, firewater, finger food and moaning helps revive us somewhat. Shadows lengthen, darkness is not far off.

"Good thing we didn't try for Paul Peak."

"Yeah, a very good thing," I say. "I couldn't't've made it anyway. You?"

"Yeah, probably," Tee says. "But I'm not real fond of darkness."

"No trail and much darkness. We know this situation very well."

"No good."

First, we see their dogs, then we hear and see Sean. Larissa is marching happily behind.

"Hey, you guys, how was it?"

Sean hurls his skis the same way Tee did: hard, into bushes. He then tosses his poles the same way Tee did. He unbuckles and pitches his pack. Larissa looks on with disapproval. She's more refined with her gear. She still likes her skis, though they're likely rock skis now.

"I probably only took them off and put them back on about one-thousand, two-hundred and eighty-seven times," Sean says. He then uses a crude expletive. "Sorry, Lar...."

She stands smiling, happy and tired.

"Here, Sean, see if this helps?"

That night there is not a great deal of conversation around the fire. Few songs are sung. Nor do we spend many cheery, warm-glow hours sharing our feelings before stumbling to our tents. And in our sleeping bags we dream of Hell: endlessly taking off, refastening; doffing and donning; stepping in and stepping out of special footwear — skis or snowshoes, snowshoes or skis — without end, repeatedly, forever, all night long. All night.

Introduction
The High Uintas

*The Uintas are a high elongate east-west
tending range consisting entirely of meta-
sedimentary and sedimentary rocks uparched
in a broad asymmetrical anticline.*
— R. E. Marsell, 1969

First you will first notice ridges, long-
stretching, above-timberline, backbone ridges. As
you get closer, you make out the cliffs, pinnacles
and individual peaks, but they are overruled by
those ridges.

The Uintas are pushed up as a curtain of
rock, not the teeth of a saw. The range forms a ruby

rise on the horizon in summer and stands cloud-white in winter. The peaks generally don't drop down to the valley floors but continue to the next rising ridge. The central ridgeline stays above 11,500 feet in elevation for ninety-some miles and forms the highest continuous ridgeline in the Lower Forty-eight. Now you know.

If it's winter, you're likely to stay away. If it is summer, at some point you will notice the multitudes of many-colored rocks: reds and purples and pinks, buffs and gray-browns. These mountains are more colorful than most of the gray granite ranges in the Rockies.

Bedrock abounds, predominately quartzite. Quartzite is metamorphic rock: Nature's twice-baked potato. Thick-formed sedimentary layers have been cooked to perfection in Earth's underground ovens. In addition to many-colored quartzite, there's also sandstone, limestone, mudstone, slate, various shales and schist. No nice gneiss here and nothing you can take for granite.

The Uinta Mountains comprise the largest and loftiest wild area in Utah. The High Uintas Wilderness Area, declared in 1984, encompasses 456,000 acres. If you add what should also be offered more protection, say, 544,00 acres of ramble-on ridges, high basins and river canyons that buttress the high country, and then double that sum by tossing in the more-accessible piedmont, you have an area as large as Yellowstone. The Uintas have a far-northern feel, as in western Montana or northwest Wyoming or north-central Alberta—a world rich in Hudsonian hyperborean alpine splendor.

Drawn in, you will find evident largeness in the landscape: big wild country ideal for dispersed recreational activities. There is a comfortable ambience in the meadows, surrounded by forest smells and shadows.

The Uintas also stand different among Rockies' ranges for an east-west orientation. From the Arctic to Tierra del Fuego, ranges display on the north-south axis. Two notable exceptions are the Uintas and Alaska's Brooks Range.

Utah is known worldwide for its fine snow and easily accessible ski areas. The Wasatch Range that stretches from Ogden to Provo, home to ten showy ski resorts, is surprisingly, only the fifth-highest mountain range in the state. The highest peak in the Wasatch, the splendid Mt. Nebo at not quite 12,000 feet, is lower than the highest peaks in the Deep Creek, Tushar, La Sal and Uinta ranges. True, the Uintas dominate numerically and in terms of elevation, but the La Sal and Tushar ranges deserve much more respect, and anyone who speaks ill of the Deep Creeks will need to step outside.

Bestowed with many high peaks, the Uintas are attractive to the peak bagger or old-style mountaineer. Summertime peak-bagging is the chief form of climbing practiced. Ski mountaineering, a clear improvement in terms of crossing talus, has yet to catch on widely, at least partly because of long approaches.

Ascensionists aim for dozens of named, poorly named and unnamed peaks, which can be hiked and scrambled (bagged) for fun and enlightenment. With a few notable exceptions, the high peaks are far from a trailhead or road. Remoteness means it takes some effort and strength of will to bag a peak, and the journey grants a true wilderness experience.

For the mountaineer, the Uintas' great benefits are elevation, remoteness, and a richness of wildlife. Talus, a collection of rock debris, is the drawback. You won't find many grassy slopes or graveled sidewalks, but you will cross many boulders.

There are some twenty peaks in the Uintas over thirteen thousand feet. The nine highest officially named are called The Notorious Nine: Kings, South Kings, Gilbert, Emmons, Lovenia, Tokewanna, Powell, Wasatch and Wilson. Notorious for good reason: each of them are separated from other peaks, prominent and committing. It took me twenty-seven years to ascend them all. One could have bagged them faster, and others surely have and will. There remain a dozen other 13,000ers, all worthy and grand.

There are other goals. Some of the Uintas most rugged peaks are over twelve thousand feet but under thirteen thousand. These are referred to as twelve-thousanders, and it's good to have a dozen or so in the fridge: Lamotte, Ostler, Spread Eagle, Agassiz, Hayden, Kletting, A-1, Beulah, North Cathedral, Dead Horse, Red Knob—but who's counting? Peak baggers count. Did I mention my over forty Uinta total peaks? I did?

Pardon my poor manners, but since peak bagging is a pursuit done in solitude, for which none but peak baggers care, it is required to boast a little, to say you did. Being able to boast about it is a good reason to do it, as good a reason as any, maybe the only good one. "I did it. Won't you allow me to talk about it?"

Returning to the Notorious Nine: Twenty-

RED STONE HEART

seven years ought to be enough to learn a thing or
two, to earn some wisdom to impart. We'll see…

Scrambling High Unita Peaks

This place has everything — every essential, every conceivable extra. It has level ground, the good grass, the wood, the easy access to water — that make a camp comfortable. It has shelter and shade, the wide views, the openness and breeziness, that raise comfort to luxuriousness. There are no mosquitos on that clifftop; there are trees shaped to the back where a man can sit and read; the ground is the coarse granular kind that produces no dust, and that, in the remote possibility of rain, would not produce mud either. Every tree has stubs of branches at the proper height for hanging things; there are enough downed logs for benches and cooking tables. And this thin air, at ten thousand feet, hits the bottom of the lungs like ether.

— Wallace Stegner, 1989,
remembering a Uinta trip to the
Granddaddy Basin in the 1920s

Part I

We Shall Gather
at the
Trailhead

1978-1983

Scrambling High Unita Peaks

Sister Dona
Finds an Activity
for
Young Kevin

*Abundance of timber on mountains
south & southwest, and beyond that plenty
of snow.*

— William Clayton
July 11, 1847

I was raised in righteousness in Holladay,
Utah, at the foot of Mt. Olympus and near Big
Cottonwood Canyon. From the backyard it was
possible to study the nearby mountains, their
seasons, moods and advantages.

Scrambling High Unita Peaks

My upbringing was reasonably strict. There wasn't much emphasis on fun in the family home but much devotion to duty. My parents tried hard to live the teachings of the Latter-Day-Saint gospel and impart wisdom unto their children. Mom and Dad had important callings in the local Ward and Stake. For youth there was a well-packed trail: church social activities and sports during the week and, of course, church on Sunday.

My mother, Dona, persuaded my practical father, Jay, that skiing might be a good activity for Young Kevin, as it would tire him out on Saturday so that he would be humbler and less fidgety on Sunday. They noted that Young Kevin seemed to have a lot of nervous energy.

A Swiss guy, Frank Sandy, ran Holladay's Matterhorn ski shop and got me geared up at the age of eight. The skis were wooden with screw-in edges, the boots leather and lace-up, and the bindings cable. He would provide the lessons.

At first the rope tow at Alta terrified me. It wanted to eat my gloves and yank my arms clean out of their sockets. The skis were long, unwieldy nightmares on my feet. I side-stepped around by myself, pouted, fretted, cried, and got lost. Frank Sandy called Sister Dona wondering where the good hell that boy is at? But after a few more lessons, and riding the chairlifts, I got to liking it.

Other people had fashionable gear, Hart Javelin skis and Koflach plastic boots, which were coveted; form-fitting black stretch pants, svelte yet burly sweaters and swanky jackets, too.

RED STONE HEART

There were a lot of rules in my parents' house: good, sensible rules to keep one on the straight and narrow. And there was surely nothing wrong with the straight and narrow, no skier would ever curse it. It was just that from an early age, I struggled with rules. I had already grown to like the wide and curvy.

All kinds of people could be found at the ski resorts, with no more goals than just having a good time. I began to feel the Calling of the Carefree Schussers: to ski on the edge of control and fly off jumps and shout about it. The packed runs, or *piste*, I learned was good. To ski on *piste* when happy or pissed off was fast and good.

Powder-privileged, I was also naturally drawn to skiing off-*piste*. In the trees or on the edges of groomed runs stretched margins of untracked snow. Watching others negotiate the untracked, and leave tracks, I wished to learn the Practices of the Powder: when to lean back and steer with the knees, when to hold the poles up and wiggle zee butt, and when to do the jump turns. In learning the Practices, the Principles were revealed: that powder isn't always there, but when it is, you must do all in your power to reach it, and then to take another run, and friends don't mean much on a powder day, and some lines you don't cross, dude.

I learned how to turn or embrace a tree, how to break trail and how to follow a trail already broken, how that making the figure eight is righteous, even with oneself, and how far one must dig to find one's gear after holding a yard-sale crash on the steep and deep. Quite importantly, I learned to fear the unexpected movement of the snow and to ascertain where and in what ways it might be expected to move.

Scrambling High Unita Peaks

Seeing that I had found something to like, my parents encouraged these outdoor interests, so long as I went to church and pretended to be good. When in church I could let my mind wander: to imagine skiing down some powder-rich bowl or scrambling up a ridge accessorized with limber pines, or also to study the girls my age and imagine not sitting in church with them. Thus, it was not too challenging to disassociate a bit when riding a pew.

Beyond the ski season, it was possible to go fishing in the Wasatch streams and lakes, and hike around just for the fun of it. The bottom of Big Cottonwood contained cliffs and boulders, easily within reach for climbing. Soon I liked being in the canyons or on the slopes more than a lot of things. I read books about the faraway ranges: the Alps, the Andes, the Himalaya.

Up in the Wasatch, looking down on Salt Lake City, with Belinda and some friends, it changed your perspective. It was easy to know which side to choose. Still, a mission calling awaited all worthy, righteous young men.

When I reached the age of accountability, I had already found a deep hankering for the home-ground canyons and forks: the glacially polished slabs, the flower-flogged meadows, the steep slopes of mountain mahogany, the shouting streams and sky-shine lakes.

Despite the waywardness, at the age of eighteen, I received a letter from the General Authorities of the Untracked, containing a call to a mission. My bosom burned and my heart swelled with joy. With tear-tinged eyes I read:

Ye shall serve in the Big Cottonwood Canyon Mission, Brighton Branch. Ye shall tract tree-to-tree with the heel fixed and free. Ye shall take the lifts and not take the lifts. Ye shall spread the Gospel of the Groomers and the Principles of the Powder.

It was an unconventional mission: no Golden Questions, no tear-tinged testimony of my love for the local people, nobody called me "Elder," but one which gave my life outdoor direction.

Thus, for some years Young Kevin labored on the snowy slopes of Big Cottonwood Canyon. In the fullness of time, he would decide that the benevolence had been enough. There were too many people in the Wasatch, even back then. He wanted to pack a track to the untracked.

On the tops of the Wasatch, at least along the eastern edge, it was possible to see the Uintas, a neighboring range, a large and more massive range, one that had to be filled with places that you just knew were hard to get to.

Young Kevin was drawn to them.

First one had to gain experience.

The Flower
&
The Waterfall

High school chums, we get ourselves geared-up locally at Kirkham's and Timberline Sports and start going backpacking in the Uintas.

1978. The plan is just to fool around for a couple hours, pack up around noon, and spend the afternoon in a leisurely walk out of the backcountry. Somebody has a wedding or something the next day, so we have to leave. We've each gone our separate ways for dawdling, the five of us: Todd, Guy, Jeffrey, myself and Lori. We have just finished high school. We share all the right ideas and opinions, just ask us. We're eighteen. About everything, we consider ourselves preternaturally omniscient. Because of our impeccable taste, to say nothing of our vast experience, it's possible that at times we might be insufferable.

Although I had had an unrequited crush on Lori four or five years before, I doubt she even noticed it. I was awkward around girls. Lori is a petite, dark-brown-eyed beauty. Nobody's honey, therefore, we can each devote our gentlemanly duty to her service. She likes the harmless attention and we like it, too.

Todd and Jeffrey are investigating some spectacular mosses and wildflowers yonder. Lori has gone off with a book to perch on some rocks and get a little sun. Guy has ventured off, camera in hand, ready to bag some images. I stay around camp, admiring my tent, New Blue, and have my journal out, ready to take down some ultra-profound thoughts about life, Nature, and the nature of life.

Guy is the one who finds her, crumpled on the talus, near the base of a waterfall, thirty-five feet down. At first he doesn't know what it is. He thinks maybe it's an old coat. But as he gets closer, he sees that it's Lori. He picks her up, carries her a couple of dozen feet to a large flat rock, checks to see that she is still breathing—she is unconscious—and runs to get us.

"Hey you guys, Lori's fallen off a cliff, and you've got to come now!"

There is fear, even terror, in his voice.

We grab first aid kits and sprint to the cliff. It's some distance from camp.

When we find her, we see that she's breathing shallowly and moaning. The back of her head is matted with blood. Her skin is blanched and clammy. Her arms and especially one elbow are scraped up but nothing's poking out. Her legs, too, seem okay, but one of her heels is torn up and the ankle seems swollen. There's blood on the rock. We know enough not to move her again, since a broken neck or back or pelvis present obvious possibilities, and the chance of internal injuries is great.

We look up at the pink-gray cliffs. She fell twenty-five, thirty, thirty-five feet? Who knows how long she's been laying on the talus? It couldn't have been more than fifteen minutes. Why had Guy just happened along to find her? We don't discuss any of this beyond the initial examination. She's breathing. She's not bleeding too much. No bones are poking out. She's got internal injuries, for sure.

There is no our friend is going to die or what should we do now? With virtually no discussion, we make a plan.

Guy and Jeffrey will go back to camp, grab daypacks with supplies, and hike out as far and as fast as they can. Maybe they can find a ranger or someone — someone to help. We don't discuss what kind of help will be needed, just help. Evacuation, of what type we do not think.

We go over our location: at the top a long talus on the main inlet to Jordan Lake, forgot to have a map to mark it on, but they'll get one back at camp, so they can tell someone, anyone, exactly where we are. This is very important. The main inlet into Jordan Lake. Above the lake, on the main inlet. The main one. Jordan Lake. This is very important. In five minutes, they're gone.

Todd and I will stay with Lori. We've had some first aide training. We're Eagle Scouts, no kidding, but we've never dealt with anything like this.

Why did she fall? It doesn't make sense. It's a perfect day with no clouds. Sure, it would have been slippery on top of the waterfall, but surely she would have known enough to stay away from the edge.

She's not wearing any shoes. Where are they?

She awakens.

Todd says, "Don't worry, we're here, Lori."

"Oh, Todd," she says.

"Where does it hurt?"

"All over," she moans.

She retches. She cries and moans. There's blood on the rock and puke. She cries and moans. Her eyes are cloudy from pain. Her skin feels hot and sweaty.

This is all very bad. Mercifully she loses consciousness again. This pattern of waking, retching, crying, moaning and falling back into her self-saving sleep is a pattern that will repeat through the day.

I'm the go-fer. We need to shade her, so I run back to get a tarp and we set it up. Then she gets cold, so I go get a sleeping bag and some pillowing clothes. Water, food, clothes, makeshift towels I fetch. I'm grateful to have something to do. The up-close is hard.

Todd stays right there. He will eventually become a medical doctor, and maybe this day he sees his calling. He holds her, cleans up her vomit, tries to calm her. He makes the difference.

I don't like the inactivity. Just waiting and watching is awful. I feel helpless and scared. I remember my little unspoken crush, how I thought that Lori and Kaye Donaldson were the hottest things around, in junior high, and I was pretty sure that I'd tried to kiss her, in the dark, outside at Kaye's house, and she'd let me, but it probably didn't mean nearly as much to her as it did to me, and now here I am, with her like this, and the crush seems a little bit indecent and beside the point, because as it events are developing, there's something out there on the edges that tells me she's going to die.

She's burning up, then chilled. Her insides hurt, she tells us, but she can't pee. Todd tells her to just pee her pants. Nothing, she can't. We know enough not to give her aspirin, because it's obvious from her blood-matted hair that she had head wounds. We want to get her to drink a little lemonade or water, but she just throws it up.

Todd holds her hands and says, "It'll be alright, Lori." And Lori says, "Oh, Todd."

All day I run between the accident site and camp. As the day wears on, it gets harder to look at him, her. She's obviously slipping and we're getting really scared. We try to make inane small talk but end up just staring at each other.

Guy and Jeffrey end up having good luck. They run into some horse people on the trail named Freckelton, from Bountiful, and they tell the horse people that our friend is going to die if we can't get her out of the mountains. There is no way she can be evacuated by horse, so the Freckeltons turn around and ride back to the trailhead. As a member of the local search and rescue, Mr. Freckelton has a radio in his outfit. (This is decades before cell or satellite phones), and if that doesn't work from the Highline Trailhead, he'll drive to Bear River Ranger Station and make arrangements for a helicopter rescue. Because if your friend is hurt as bad as you say, that's the only way we can save her.

They assure them that she's hurt that bad. She fell thirty, thirty-five feet.

The accident has happened well within the wilderness boundary, and helicopters are not allowed in wilderness areas. There are two exceptions, however, in the case of rescue and in the case of fire suppression. In other circumstances, we would not have had much in common with the Freckletons, nor they us, but in this situation, they are miraculous.

They also run into a wilderness ranger. He too has a radio. He'll check out the victim, render necessary assistance, and confirm via his radio.

We don't know of any of these plans until the wilderness ranger shows up. He's a young guy, not much older than we are, and he is utterly useless.

We have Lori shaded, blanketed and stabilized as best we could, he notices. He does no more than an extremely brief exam. He doesn't even touch her. Best to wait for the doctors, he says. He also tells us that he can't stand the sight of blood. In fact, it looks like he's about to faint.

He retreats over to a slope where he can get radio reception, tries to make his calls, and then goes down to the shore of the lake to eat his lunch.

Lori, meanwhile, is fading. Her skin is a pale shiny yellow-bluish color; her pupils are dilated and unfocused; her pulse is rapid and shallow. We feel certain she has internal injuries, but there's nothing more we can do.

Jeffrey and Guy pass the wilderness ranger as they stagger back to us sometime after 4:00 p.m.

I make one last trip back to camp to fetch some ground pads to use to make an **X** to guide the helicopter in landing.

We wait. We fret.

Happy sound at last. We see the Life Flight chopper come over the north shoulder of Mt. Agassiz. The big bird touches down on top of the cliff by the waterfall. They'd gone to the wrong place first, they said.

We help the nurse and doctor get the litter down the cliff and talus and watch as they examine her. IV in, just in time, they say. They slice open her shirt to attach the heart monitor. We pick her up gingerly and get her in the litter. The strapping in seems to take forever. Even with six of us it's hard work to carry her up over the talus and hummocks to the bird. She pukes part way there. We roll her over and clean it up. She cries about her stomach. And who could blame her for the moaning and tears and puke, poor little broken thing. The doc said she had been lucky that we'd been there and that we'd done the right things.

The helicopter takes off, and we wave and hug each other. She'll be in the ER in maybe twenty-five minutes. She'll make it, we hope.

It seems like eighty miles we walk back to the trailhead that night. It's too much effort even to talk. And yet somehow we make it out, pushed on by the notion that for once, and at least once, if only a lucky once, we did the right things, and we know it.

And we learn, too, that mountains can kill you in a minute.

RED STONE HEART

When we visit her in the hospital, some of the health care workers look at us suspiciously, as if we'd had a hand in how beaten-up she looks. Her recovery takes months but years later we go backpacking together at Canyonlands. She walks with perhaps a little hitch in her get along, but that she walks at all and wants to backpack is amazing.

Postscript: Forty years later, at a high school reunion after party, I share this chapter because Todd, Guy, Jeffrey, myself and Lori are all there. We share memories and give mutual thanks that it turned out the way it did. Lori looks great, still spry and daring. She's a proud grandmother today, so that surely matters. And the rest of us still have our hair and most of our faculties. The only thing she wants me to do vis a vis the public is to list all of her injuries for the record. The main ones include the fully fractured pelvis and two cracked vertebrae; a grade 3 concussion, sprained ankle, and foot fracture; significant internal bruising and some lacerations of organs and tracts; and many cutaneous contusions and abrasions.

Hike, Scramble, Climb

To give each pursuit its proper name, hiking involves using only one's legs as primary locomotive source, whether on-trail or off. If a person fancies using poles to pretend he or she is skiing while walking, that is still hiking.

Climbing involves the use of both hands and feet to ascend rock, snow or ice at distances where a fall would cause much harm. That is to say, one's boot soles are off the deck. Hands and feet on the rock, butt out or in. Climbing is made safer by using ropes. Attached to the rock with a variety of devices, ropes are used to catch a climber, to limit the length and seriousness of falls. Falls are to be avoided, certainly, but a rope, hardware and harness make some falls routine. On a rock face or ridge, on cliffs, on steep snow and ice, a climber carries a rope and uses it often.

RED STONE HEART

Scrambling is somewhere between hiking and climbing, and a combination of both. It can be seen as climbing without a rope. On baggable peaks it is often or fairly short duration and milder consequences. Maybe a few steep boulders on a face. Perhaps a little crack or friction up a ridge. A snowfield rather than a glacier. A bear crawl up some talus. A boulder problem or two. A gendarme (rock tower) to skirt or disarm.

On peaks or routes the decision to scramble or climb is usually made beforehand. To carry a rope and gear means a heavier pack. An un-carried rope is never used. Also, with scrambling an easier route is often chosen.

In the Uintas, there's lots of hiking, some climbing, and there can be quite a bit of scrambling on peaks and getting to them.

Tungsten

My car is a sporty Plymouth Scamp.

Orange of hue, accented by white racing stripes—not to mention the white vinyl roof, scalloped back window, and swank wheel covers—the Sporty Scamp is living proof of what ails the American auto industry in the year of its manufacture, 1970, and what should have.

The Scamp is the short-lived "sporty" version of the reliable Plymouth Valiant. Gutless and wandering, this two-doored death trap has one outstanding characteristic: an inline six-cylinder power plant that will survive anything. You can't kill a Valiant. Even Hell's Canyon, with its many rocky chicanes, sand traps and steeplechase impediments, shakes the Sporty One to the limit but doesn't throw her Sportiness off stride. Nor do the tires deflate. "That's why this lady drives a Scamp."

RED STONE HEART

At the top of Hell's Canyon, Jeffrey Floor and I roll scampily through forest on narrowing roads to what we hope is the trailhead. It is unmarked and our map is not very good. In fact, we have a good map only of the Kings Peak area, but that's twenty-five miles away from here, so we roll on hope, innocence and a vague guidebook. We set off on what we guess is the right trail under threatening clouds. We head north. We're still eighteen.

In the current era, nearly everyone who aims at Kings Peak starts on the North Slope (rather than the South Slope) for a variety of good reasons. The trail starts relatively high, stays fairly high, and with fifteen miles of gentle inclines and several rock-ridden steeps, leads to the prize, the high point of the Beehive State. It is thronged with pilgrims in season. Thronged! The southern approaches are far longer, rockier, less trammeled.

In picking the southern route in 1978, we are not familiar with these considerations. All we think we want is a good, long backpack that starts over ten thousand feet and passes many lakes.

It's well after Labor Day, though, so sharing the wilderness with others is largely eliminated. In fact, we will be out for seven days and we will see no other people. Not even a single solitary human being. Nobody.

Grandson of immigrants from Crete, Jeffrey's a bit of misfit in Holladay, Utah. Also, his dad, a

Scrambling High Unita Peaks

World War Two veteran, perished in an accident when Jeffrey was only four months old, so he has a better reason, perhaps, for being an odd ball than I do, but we'll call it a tie, a matched pair. We are both comfortable with senseless repetition within the novelty of the Cosmos. I may have threatened him with a stick because I'd had enough, and all he could say was, "Why don't you want me to sing?" We're young, nutty and fit but not athletic.

From Five Points Lake it is yet a long way to Kings Peak. Perhaps it would be good to carry one more day and get closer. Perhaps it would not. We decide to rest a day and then go for it.

On the summit day, guessing it will be a long one, Jeffrey and I make an early start. We gird our loins. We walk. We also walk and then again we walk. Me and Floor, Floor and I. We have to cross a high basin, gain Tungsten Pass, traverse the upper Yellowstone, take the yak path up to Anderson Pass, then hop Death Platters to the top of the state. That's just half of the itinerary. We repeat it for return.

We spend the entire day above timberline. We sweep past willows turned red and yellow, over gold and russet grassy hummocks. We pass boulders big as horses, big as big-ass trucks, big as houses, big as mansions, all grainy buff and rosy, tattooed with mustard-colored lichen, striped with improbable touches.

Ice is already filigreed in the bogs and stream sides. All day hurrying, all the livelong day. The indigo sky stretches, none too warm. Winter comes early to the high country. The yak path is greasy brown and schisty. It's fairly warm on the summit.

RED STONE HEART

On top we gaze down upon the drainages, nothing we have ever imagined before, big heaps of rocks and dark forests and whopping distances. We can see sixteen lakes. We are the highest snotty boys in Utah. While it's good to be on top, our beds lie many miles away.

Later, we also feel a sudden onrush of the late-day fear.

Although it has been pleasant to re-cross the russet hummocks, to salute the big pretty red and pink rocks, to swish past many acres of yellow willows, just about Tungsten time we realize that despite being really quite frankly tired we must run. Or at least trot. A night out in September's cold embrace at over eleven thousand feet is not something we can support.

Trot we do. Trot we will.

Welcome to the idea that a night out is a bad idea.

Welcome to the idea that many things must be done to make sure this does not happen.

Learn how the desperate mania kicks in and pushes you on, makes you really feel alive.

It's about two-times farther on the way back. We reach Five Point close to inky. It has suddenly gotten very cold. Just all of a sudden very cold and nearly all dark.

At camp Jeffrey is too knackered to do anything but engage with his sleeping bag. I'm not far behind but hungry. I cook soup with whatever canned meat we have. My goodness but the soup tastes good. He spills nearly the whole bowl on his sleeping bag, mops it up with a t-shirt, falls asleep a-mumble. It kind of scares me.

Scrambling High Unita Peaks

Somewhere is left the impression, the way fear urges you on across the golden meadows, sharpening things up as the light gilds and shadows stretch and safety is yet some distance away. It is somehow right, though bordering on wrong. Right is warm under layers. Wrong is somewhere out in the dark and cold.

You carry right and make yourself ready for it.

,

That was the positive, good side of pushing it, but in the early days, there were other people I nearly killed.

One time, Guy Wheelwright and I brought the splendid Elaine Alexis McBride along for some early season skiing above Alta. None of us was very good at backcountry skiing then, though Guy and I had downhill skied a lot. Alexis was a rank beginner, but richly endowed with pulchritude, and, well, in form-fitting blue jeans and a fringy leather jacket, with suede gloves, we'd take her anywhere she wanted. We talked about how far we'd gone but just kept wanting to go up. The problem was not going up but going down, and we had to get back down on edgeless wonders and low-cut boots.

Miss Elaine fell repeatedly until she was soaked and mighty cold. At sunset hypothermia and shock set in, and we were a long way from the parking lot. Her fair skin turned bluish, her lips showed ice, and she was shivering uncontrollably.

Half dragging and carrying her, Guy and I came upon a cabin that the owner left unlocked in case of this very eventuality, and after quite a bit of treatment, hot drinks, bed sharing and some wrestling, we were able to get her warmed up and stabilized.

This was not a good strategy for dating. She could have died, and we would have been the ones responsible.

On another occasion in the High Sierra while backpacking with another high school chum, Tori Shoulders, and her husband Rob, I got to meet hypothermia again.

Rob mentioned that he was susceptible to hypothermia and altitude sickness, but the higher we hiked, the better he felt, and being by nature competitive, he wanted to just keep going.

Camp was set up at over ten thousand feet, and the afternoon was progressing nicely, when Rob started to slip. By then I knew the signs of shock and hypothermia. Tori in his sleeping bag with him couldn't warm him. Hot drinks weren't doing any good. In addition to the pallor, he was complaining about a splitting headache. It left us with no choice.

We packed up as fast as we could and headed downhill as darkness fell. Sierra trails are steep, and by the time we got below 8700 feet, he'd made remarkable improvement.

I reflected on these close calls. To some degree there was human error, and some of the error was mine. I also grappled with the notion that although seemingly benign, the backcountry world possessed a certain amount of inherent danger. The people I had been with weren't very experienced, and although one gains experience through experience, I didn't really want to experience someone dying on my watch.

Personally, I thought it would be a good idea to get some more training in outdoor program courses or clinics or clubs, with more experienced climber/skiers. I didn't, but I thought it was a good idea. I did meet some budding alpinists who had the same interests and we acted as each other's guides.

Meet, Greet Mel Talus

If you should choose to ascend an Uinta peak, you will meet with talus. Ordinary talus and Mel Talus. Mel Talus and the Big Rollers. Mel Talus with the Death Platters. The Mortality Makers featuring Mel T. All kinds of talus placed in the way of your goal, broken up and scattered about.

On your way you will cross much talus. Some talus is okay, much talus is not. Loose, broken up, unstable, rolling and easy-to roll, sliding, dusty, schisty, wobbly, rain-soaked and slippery, frozen-in-place-and-deadly, talus. You will meet and greet slopes of talus, faces full or talus, gullies rich in talus, cliffs decked with talus, ridges and their gendarmes strewn with talus. Scree is small and gravelly, talus is large and bouldery. Talus is temptation. With talus there is little redemption. It's small-scale mass wasting.

All mountain ranges contain talus. The Uintas just contain more of it. Blame a dozen epochs of glaciation, blame the hard durability of the quartzite rock, at some point on talus you will have no one to blame but yourself. You chose it, you hate it, now you have to get through it.

Go on snow or on the talus you will go.

The Wall
of the
Mountain King

This is how I get to know Mark Alpenglow.

1980. By the time we reach Amethyst Lake other members of our party—Lizard Man Steve, Sulieman the Magnificent and Stephanie B.—are intent on angling or dawdling. This new guy, Mark, is roommates with Steve. We talk a bit. We're not here to fish. We have neither license nor tackle.

Mark is newly arrived from Buffalo, New York, because his brother came to Salt Lake for college. Mark's clearly the kid brother who is way wilder than the staid Richard, a fine arts painter.

Mark is a big guy, with a big attitude and big voice he doesn't mind using. Added to that is large red hair and overdone sideburns covering pale, freckled skin. He seems vaguely Canadian, like your nightmare loud uncle from Thunder Bay. He's not the kind to want to turn around if the going gets rough. He has no experience but wants to get into mountaineering.

As we watch the others ready their fishing gear, Mark and I can't help but look up at the northeast face of Ostler Peak. It rises directly and steeply from the lakeside to the summit. It looms. The closer we look, we see that on the right side of the central crease there are some solid-looking moderate-angle cliffs that might provide a rocky ladder up.

In alpinism the most direct route is considered to receive high style points. The Italian word for this is *direttissima,* which is the sort of word one wields in campfire conversation in the climber bars of Chamonix, Zermatt and Jackson Hole. The *direttissima* wastes no time in the back and forth but prefers a straight line, which is often also the shortest route, often also the most sheer.

Mark and I decide to go.

There are no snowfields or ice fields on Ostler Peak in August. Instead, for slipperiness there is yellow-gray talus, and we flail up plenty of it. We grope toward more solid rock. The cliffs are brown and less slippery than the slopes. Nor are they exactly vertical, but nicely steep, full of hand and footholds. We make good time up the face and first cliffs.

It's scary but fun. We are old-style mountaineers. We tighten our laces. We scramble. We don't talk much, lost in the labor.

RED STONE HEART

The crux is a brown-purple cliff, higher than the rest, with loose-rock gullies on either side. Terrain makes the choice simple: stay out of the gullies. We start up it. I lead, Mark follows.

On a narrow ledge, or out on a face, when the hand or footholds aren't quite big enough, the climber or scrambler can get scared or "gripped" with fear. When this happens, an involuntary physical response occurs: the legs begin to move up and down like the business-end of a sewing machine. This involuntary response comes at exactly the worst time. Out on the steep and gnarly, it's much better to remain calm and collected. But the "sewing-machine legs" fire up. It is for this reason that people sometimes plummet from the side of mountains.

Another name for this is "The Berninas," so-called for a brand of sewing machine named for some snowy peaks near St. Moritz.

As I look down at Mark, I can see that his legs are making like the bobbin and thread.

Speaking of thread, when a climber is roped, and the Berninas come on, and they do, the rope is there to catch him or her. This is why using a rope is often a good idea. We have no rope, of course, so I tell him that it's not too bad, take a deep breath, and we'll be done with this cliff pretty soon.

One way to bring on the Berninas is to look down. There's just something about, say, eighty or ninety feet of air-to-ground, or a couple of hundred, or several hundred, or a thousand, that can shake things up, start the knees to knock past each other like strangers in Grand Central Station.

Another way to get gripped is when your partner gets gripped. It's contagious. You can pass it around.

So, while Mark is beset with the Berninas, I can't look down and I can't wait around. I push on and tell him to do the same.

He uses some bad language and says, "This is where I'm going to get hurt." He says it calmly and composedly, as though he's watching himself.

Now when I look down, I see that on his ledge he's sewing a wedding dress, replete with many doilies and sashes: an elaborate wedding dress, a dainty veil and a very impressive train.

Sew, boy, sew.

"Don't look down, just straight ahead and up," I urge.

"This is where I'm going to get hurt," he says.

"Come on…you've got it."

The angle lessens the higher I go. I shout that it gets easier.

Pretty soon I've topped the cliff and reach out for talus, suddenly preferring a slippery slide to free falling. Mark grunts his way up, pale and green-tinged.

"Oh my goodness," he says. "Me no like."

"No?"

"No," he says. "ME NO LIKE."

"Cliffs give you fear?"

"Yes, much fear. Me fall long way."

There is one last clifflet. Passing over this false summit and circumventing a deep rocky trench, we stand on top of Ostler Peak, 12,718 feet. We are happy with ourselves and the world. The sun beams. Nearly no clouds mar the perfect sky.

We holler.

We roll some rocks down the central crease of the north-east face. We smell the way the rocks do when they break up in plummets of dust and clatter.

RED STONE HEART

We cackle. We giggle. It is good to roll rocks. They make noise and smell spicy.

Behind us a gigantic basin yawns, lake-bestraggled and meadow-strewn. We see at least a dozen blue diadems, watery jewels, way down there. We can see Mt. Timpagnosis and the Wasatch to the west. We make out Mt. Nebo. We are hundreds of feet higher. To the east in our range, big gray peaks burl up: Cleveland, Explorer and Squaw. A few afternoon puffy clouds sail around the Wyoming plains. We do a self-timer shot, grinning through our lengthy hair and manifest whiskers.

Skiers' right of the central gully, we plunge down a face of gravel and dirt, sending up clouds of dust. We spread apart and go down at the same time so we don't knock rocks down on each other. We are wearing sneakers, not so good in dusty conditions. Toward the bottom, we veer away from the face and onto gray, brown and purple talus fields.

Back at the lake, Lizard Man Steve and Suleiman the Magnificent hoist stringers of fine brookies for their labors. Amethyst Lake surrenders some lovely ones to show for an afternoon of productive idleness. Stephanie has wandered off bringing back a bower of flowers, very pretty and pretty. We salute our trophy too, rearing behind us, notched not taken. Ostler Peak. *Cha-ching.* It is good we are all so happy.

Less so as the misery-tinged miles to the car stretch into evening. Eventually, back down in the forest, we cannot see our heavenward monolith of the day, but feel it has left its impressions on us. Mark and I are thoroughly whipped by it, but as we plod, too tired to talk, we have become aware of a new range of possibilities, what good things can be done in a long day, and we know the desire to reach out for a big slice of them. Not every day, but some days. Some great days. Some cloudy days.

Part II
Where the Peaks
Have No Names

1986-1988

When you were young
and skied the chutes,
how did it feel
in leather boots?

—"But Only Crud" after Neil Young

General Disaster, Tee Trundler, Dr. Alpenglow

Dirtbags

I find my band.

I'd like to begin with my hair, the way I feel about my hair. Hair is in the air. Hair is everywhere.

At times in the 1980s I wear my hair long and curly and often sport a beard after the granola dirtbag wild man fashion of the day. True, I prefer close-cropped New Wave and punk to the hairy classic rock, but I can advertise granola dirtbag wild manly-ness by sporting a somewhat-billowing freak flag. You got a problem with that?

In these days the long hair is required for a budding alpinist. Reinhold Messner is just now climbing the highest mountains in the world as Reinhold-with-his-Hair-always-with-Him, and in good style, and without bottled oxygen, and one wants to emulate. For sure I want to find some dudes and dudettes with whom to disport in the wilderness, some buds who share the will to gnarl.

Fortunately, while at the Norwegian University of Utah I encounter a variety of like-minded souls. We meet on outdoor program trips, in the dorms, at parties, at trailheads. Pretty soon we have a regular gang. We decide to form a band but not a hair band and not a boy band.

Well…. Singing is the gateway, or at least vocalizing. Singing, you see, increases the *esprit d'corps*, and you can't deny it.

We sing irreverent versions of songs when we drive to hikes or tours or climbs. We sing during down time for no good reason. When the mojo is working, we croon. We sing while skiing, using our two poles as double-necked guitars, if necessary. We sing mainly rock and roll, but sometimes we are the Temptations and sometimes we are the Pips. Now and then we noodle along with prog rock and consider concept albums.

Generally, we try to stick to the written melodies, with broad free interpretations, especially for the chance for extended "doodle-dee-dos," but we change all the words to fit what we do. End rhymes with "ski," "poofder" "beer," "shank," "hoar," "poles," "rope," "crud," "horses," "pig," "car," "Arctic Cat," are not hard to manage, yet still vaguely highbrow.

Poofder calling from the avalanche zone; forget it brother, you can go it alone.

(Note: In British parlance, *poofder* is a slur for an overly flamboyant individual. Here it is used as a more mellifluous alternative to "powder.")

In a moment of shocking punk immaturity we

call ourselves the Dead Babies. Wait, let me explain. It's only because we had found a sacred amulet, an inch-long cute little resin baby doll embedded in the asphalt of the Harmon's Grocery parking lot on the eve of our first big trip together, an expedition to the Wind Rivers in 1981, saw it as a totem, and took it along with us. It could have been anything. We were searching for identity. Good wine takes a long time to age.

Once Dead Babies, we further bestow ourselves with stage names: Astral Bounder, General Disaster, Don Juan, Suleiman the Magnificent, Larry Darkness, Dr. Alpenglow, Lizard Man Steve, Captain Sandstone (yours truly), and Tee Trundler. We aspire to be more than just singing alpinists. We develop our skills. Terrible as it is, it suits. We're not mature. We learn the ropes and scales.

With willing accomplices, it becomes easy to scare up someone in winter to go and find some backcountry poofder to furrow. Spring means much of the same and peak bagging. Summer involves backpacking or river trips. Fall is a shoulder season: trips to the desert or high country until the flakes fly, our idealized calendar.

Women we often thought of diligently, and respectfully, and we spoke of their many qualities with immoderate adoration, and we tried to get closer to share our feelings with them but had only slim luck in bringing love interests along on adventures, for crystal-clear reasons. What self-respecting potential paramour would want to spend even the slightest amount of time with these Peter Pans? What do they do for fun? A slide show…. Talk about what they're going to do? Bor-ing!

And worse, let's mention the tedious

self-absorption, the boasting, the obvious thrill to be with danger. Fetishizing the fear and gear. What's with the pointy hats and silly slippers? Great catch? Not!

We try and learn that doing somewhat-less-gnarly things with potential amorous friends is a better strategy than trying to kill someone on a date.

While studying at the Norwegian, several of us share a house on Le Grand Street in Salt Lake City. Mark is working on the university grounds crew and becomes our emcee because he's enthusiastic and loud.

While most of the Dead Babies are introverted, Mark can be encouraged to be very outgoing. By nature, he displays an outspoken mien common to many of the Empire State persuasion. His opinions he is not shy to share. His opinions he regards as accepted fact, and accepted fact should always be shared. He interprets a variety of songs from Genesis and Pink Floyd and sides with Syd. He doesn't belong to one particular critical school. He isn't shy about expressing his opinions about football, especially regarding the Buffalo Bills. He smokes Merits and whatever else there is around. He likes drinking.

What he lacks in experience and natural skills (balance, judgement, route-finding, turning ability) he makes up with mania and summit drive. Liking to be on top, he becomes the Permanent Interim President and Fearless Leader of the Peak-A-Week Club and seeks to live up to its name. One week, one peak.

His list soon grows and he gives himself a gold medallion and "Dr. Alpenglow" as stage name. He proves himself willing to know the peaks at times of fading light, the alpenglow of yellow, peach and rose.

In these days it seems finding solitude with one's crew is possible in every canyon and any fork of the Wasatch. Salt Lake City hasn't yet been discovered by loads of people just like us. Loads of shiny, fit and happy people who will buy good gear and learn all the good places to shred, many of whom will share the will to gnarl.

And if it seems too crowded, we opt for the Uintas.

Briefly, while we're on this topic, this is a golden, better time before snowboarding: blessed years before the young walrus hordes flop about seated on slopes, slap-slamming their planks as part of the elaborate mating ritual. Rides? Hey friend, skiers ski and no one rides on snow. One rides donkeys, floats in a parade or Harleys.

This is a time when the snow-kissed heights are solely the realm of the pure in spirit, two plankers on boards so thin you can hardly see 'em. Those who use the same equipment (skis) to go both uphill and down, who touch the snow only when they fall, and who wax or skin for grip and glide. The 1980s — the golden age of powder and pinheads, granola dirtbag wild men and wild women in Andean hats and Mother Karen jackets in search of powder up to and including the yin yang and face shots in West Bowl. I kinda miss it.

Pardon me, but nobody says nothing then about any Olympics except in jest. No bribes have been given to ensure the bid. No facilities are constructed at taxpayer expense. No banners are draped from downtown buildings. No fires are lit within. Few have heard of Mitt Romney or imagined his rakish beret. Few have had the earthly vision of Mitt gliding in on his white bobsled to save the games. Or that the glide would be a prelude for a run at the White House. Or that riding the white bobsled must have strengthened his latent backbone, giving him the inner strength to torment Pres. Pinocchio.

Sorry, I got sidetracked on winter. Summer is three months of bad skiing and good mountaineering.

True, most of us don't have steady loving acquaintances, for obvious reasons, and so sublimate our impulses into getting out and getting on top as often as we can. Sure, I dream about finding some honey-toned soulmate with whom to share adventures on the sharp edge, perhaps even the will to gnarl, and short of that, just someone who is into nature and likes to get out, and I swear I can change, no really, but in the meantime there is the boy band, the Dead Babies, and chasing after dancers. And dancers aren't going to want to go out and slog some peak.

For social fun we do have the Figments: Keri, Shari, Lori, Sinovi and Mary, five female Dead Heads who are good for the scenery, who never turn down an invitation to party, and who always leave a scent of patchouli as they waft on to the next shindig. A serious and meaningful relationship with any of the Figments doesn't seem likely.

If we want to change anything, we want to go higher and farther.

Before court proceedings begin, the LeGrand House will break up. Most of the DBs stay in SLC for a while.

RED STONE HEART

Alpenglow will eventually settle in Logan, Utah, attend Utah State University and earn a degree in wildlife biology. He continues his studies, working on a master's, but on the breaks, he can be found crashing at one Babies' house or another.

For many weeks in the summers of 1986 and '87 Dr. Alpenglow and I find time to bag peaks and nothing else. We go on a spree. We engage in a peak-bagging extravaganza and overdo it in the Uintas. We do it for fun and because too much of "real" life is littered with stupid boundaries, beset with crevasses of conformity. We bag peaks like there is no tomorrow.

Three Thousand
Four Thousand

If the goal of the game is to reach the top of a mountain, then there need to be some rules, some yardstick, to quantify and qualify an objective, as well as measures to use to evaluate its significance, and perhaps something to argue about. This can be an objective practice once criteria for the peak itself are established. The ascent's style can be evaluated by the number of miles one must walk to reach the base, the amount of vertical gain of the peak, the overall difficulty of the tour, and limbs lost in the process.

How high does a peak have to be to count as a worthy ascent?

Fortunately, our outdated Imperial height and length measuring system (feet, miles) matches the Metric System in two key numbers. Since mountaineering as a recreational activity began in Europe, deciding an evaluative criteria developed there as well. Early it was possible to see that three thousand meters was a magical number. Timberline is much lower in the Alps, but the good stuff starts often at this point, three thousand meters, nearly exactly equivalent to our ten thousand feet. (By "our" I mean as it relates to the Rocky Mountains.)

To make a long story short, ten thousand feet is a crucial number for a real, worthy peak you can boast about, put on your list or scorecard, or stick a push pin in the map on your wall. Granted, three thousand meters is 9842 feet, allowing an opening for dispute. All you're likely to end up with is special pleading over 158 feet. Ten thousand feet is much easier to think about and remember.

You've got to start somewhere, and though there be hills and peaks, cliffs and summits lower than this in the Rockies, (yet alarmingly grand and worthy of attention and reverence) ten thousand is close to timberline. At or near timberline the landscape is often suddenly much more majestic and altitude sickness begins to strike.

Altitude sickness is no joke. The body acclimates or adjusts to differences in altitude only a thousand vertical feet per day on average. This means you might get sick on Rainier or trying for Whitney.

This means that you better be prepared.

Also, it must be said, to tip a brim to John Denver, the Rocky Mountain natural high occurs right here, ten thousand feet, not 9842. Hell yes, you can tell the difference: 9842 is "Aye, Calypso" with French mariners in speedos and beanies, not the

Scrambling High Unita Peaks

Rocky Mountain High (RMH) dispensed at the big Ten-Oh.

Sorry. The next demarcation is four thousand meters or about thirteen thousand feet. In the Rockies and in the Alps, generally, four-thousanders or thirteeners demand commitment, and are a more serious undertaking involving training, experience, approach walking and special gear. A thirteener is nearly always worth mentioning.

The United States of America boasts many states with peaks topping ten thousand feet. Alaska has over ninety, and Hawaii has two thirteeners and a ten-thousander.

In reference to another elite category of majesty, Colorado is nobly endowed with the lion's share of the fourteen-thousand-foot peaks, dozens of them, with California showing golden and glimmering a bracelet of her own. And let's not forget the great and powerful Rainier, standing bulbous and gurgling outside Seattle.

Utah and Wyoming's pride are their thirteeners, from the Grand Teton to Fremont, Gilbert to Wind River. California and Colorado boast numerous thirteeners, of course, and Nevada and New Mexico also make this club, barely. That's the Super Six. Here's to you!

Right here, though, let's pause for a moment to celebrate the great twelve-thousander peaks of the Rockies. There's surely a lot of them! In such a party, Idaho, Montana, and Arizona get the first dance and Washington gets the second. And of the myriad eleven-thousanders, Mt. Hood earns highest marks for beauty and symmetry, for if ever a hill could do a state proud, then hats off for Hood of Oregon.

The consequence of this is that all eleven

of the Western states boast peaks that count: protuberances that rise higher than the magical marker, ten thousand feet, and our two Pacific siblings do, too.

This means that anyone living in a western state can be a peak bagger on home ground.

Still, when you're walking with your buddy up the West Fork of Black's Fork, deep within the North Slope of the Uintas, and it's raining, it makes you feel low, even if your buddy is Dr. Mark Alpenglow. You wonder and wait as spruces drip and you see nothing but clouds on cliffs. How long will it last? How far can we go? The only thing you know is that you're not going to take the trouble to turn around.

A Sudden Discharge
of
Atmospheric Electricity

*The earliest geological induction of
primeval man is the doctrine of terrestrial
catastrophe. This ancient belief has its roots in
the actual experience of man, who himself has
been witness of certain terrible and destructive
exhibitions of sudden, unusual telluric energy...*

*Catastrophism is therefore the survival of
a terrible impression upon the very substance of
human memory.*

—Clarence King, 1877

RED STONE HEART

1986. We've been walking up steep meadows thick with grass sodden with yesterday's rain.

There isn't much discussion as we crest out at Red Knob Pass. First, we backtrack west half-a-mile and take care of Red Knob Peak, scarcely higher than the pass, but named and measured, 12,248 feet. It lends its name to a United States Geological Survey (USGS) quad map, one of the finest USGS quads.

Back at Red Knob Pass, we are presented with two very high peaks, whose names we do not know, but whose prominence is plainly evident. One is closer than the other, and it rears up as a magnificent beckoning whale back, or really more of a shark's fin, bulging as it narrows upward, boldly thrusting. We pick it, and we get underway.

(Later we will learn its name is Wasatch Peak, 13,156, thirty-three feet above four thousand meters.)

Alpenglow and I cover the crazy-colored undulating schisty terrain to the peak's base, running on the downhill stretches, studying the cliff band that guards the shark's fin as we go. Once we find a way through the cliffs, we'll be golden. The south ridge will definitely go, with plenty of air surrounding it, and no flat sections.

As we start up through the cliff bands, it cannot be said that we don't see the clouds. No, the clouds are abundantly evident, right over there. The peaks to our west are already socked in. The horizon that way is darkly laden with moisture.

There won't be any running on Wasatch's south ridge, though. It's nothing but medium-sized blocks, steeply laid, sharp and slippery. It is steep, rising a thousand feet in half-a-mile.

Scrambling High Unita Peaks

Precipitation changes with altitude. In the lowlands clouds usually drop rain, while up high they spit snow, even in July and August, sometimes especially in July and August.

Snow begins to swirl as we struggle up the gray-green shark-fin ridge, the slippery staircase. At one point I pass the fossil of a fern, a big old fossil fern, slick on green quartzite. It impresses itself on me, having been impressed and pressed: olive drab on light green rock. It's an ancient fern sodden with a surface of slush, a fern that grew perhaps half a billion years ago, A fern that grew and died, and was covered with sand, sand that was subsequently turned to stone and then baked over countless millennia, and pushed up to these crystalline heights. It's impossible to grasp for its greenness, the greenness of the rocks, or the history of its uplift. I holler to Mark about the fern.

He says, "Forget the effing fern."

It's no time to stop. No time to pause at a fern bar. No time to grasp any of that flinging away. Upward we push.

We face big swirling snowflakes sourced from the steady west wind. I'm thinking this is a bad place to be in a blizzard. This is a really bad place to be in a blizzard. This is a blizzard. Therefore, this is a bad, a really bad place to be.

Some summit. We barely make it out in the whiteout. All we can do on top is curse and turn around. Will we be able to find the way back down? We plunge into the whirling maelstrom. Endlessly the boulders spill down, trout-slippery.

To speak of lightning: if it's close, you smell it just before you feel it. It begins with the scent of busting rocks, the sharp, grainy stink of it.

Granules of fear sprout on the tongue. You hear a palpable WHOOSH. Then you see solid white and nothing but white, as though someone switched on a thousand spotlights in the middle of bright-white blizzard day. A nanosecond later, a loud-chained terrifying unraveling begins, like ripping the skin off the sky.

Crick, Crick, Crick. WHAM!

The shockwave of avalanche airblast knocks my feet out from under me. I land on snow. There's a terrible ringing, a sharp stench. It's a knock-down punch.

I'm cowering on the snow-coated rocks, hardly able to move. I'm going to die. It was right overhead, the bolt. Wasn't I just electrocuted? No, I'm alive but kneeling in the snow, knees poking into rocks, ultra-gripped and pants pissing.

Am I alone? I thought I saw someone. Someone up here? Over there. I see him again. Alpenglow. He's cowering, flopping. He's moving. He can't be dead.

"Hey, what do we do now?" I yell into the blizzard.

"Let's get the hell out of here!"

We get up and go in slow-mo, stumbling. We are in the open on snow-coated rocks, hundreds of feet below the summit but not yet down the cliffs. Zeus-the-Thunderer will not miss next time. There are bullseye circles on our backs.

The air crackles with threat. Lightning scrapes cloud to cloud, above us, around us.

Concentrating, tunnel-visioned, we make for the cliffs. We're lunging forward and doing the robot dance. Another one cracks the sky.

SHAAASSSSHHHH.

Crick, Crick, Crick. KABOOM!

The cliff. How we get down the cliff is simple. Poor rock climbers each, utter fear induces us to make nice, crisp, clean balletic moves. We make it to the bottom, cringing as we go.

Down at last on undulating shale, we briefly look at each other. We do not talk but share the same thought. We take to our legs. We run. We are machines. We are scared. We run a couple of hundred yards down the ridge. There is further crackling.

We see a gully open up on the right. Its secrets are obscured by mist. More rumbles. We leap into it. Even if the gully cliffs out, even if we have to traverse a blue schisty ledge half-way to Mountain View, Wyoming, we are not stopping. We plunge into the seeming safety of the mud-socked gully.

Sliding and riding down the slippery slopes, in steady rain, huge clumps of clay on our soles, over talus, gravel, scree, schist: legs burning, lungs burning, hearts a-pumping, in poor light and pouring rain, we descend.

Sweat-drenched and utterly shagged we reach the first trees. They are not tall enough to give the illusion of safety. We go on until we reach the first groves, and then we go just a little bit farther.

Rain clouds lift. At last beneath fairly-tall trees we rest.

After a while: "Um, did you know it was totally stupid, what we did there," I say.

"What was?"

"What?"

"Yes, what specifically?" he asks. "Did you say stupid?"

"What?" I say. "Okay, let's start with the up and the down."

"Boy, it's good to be back down here," he says. "Isn't it, though? Nice trees, nice little trees, really nice cute little trees."

"We damn near died."

"We did," he says. "...I suppose."

"Gonna remember that one," I say.

He looks at his gloves. "Are you saying it wasn't very schmart?" he says.

"No, it wasn't very schmart. Can't get no closer, Alpenglow."

"No closer."

"Closer than LaMotte, for sure."

"Yes," he says. "Closer than LaMotte and not schmart."

"I had an uncomfortable feeling," he says. "But it's gone now." He fiddles around.

I stand up and stretch. The peaks are still socked in.

"Next time we'll go faster," he says.

"We couldn't go any faster...are you kidding me, we ran, both ways."

"Sometimes going fast is schmarter," he says.

"Next time," I say. "How about we don't do it, next time?"

"That's one solution," he says. "There might be others."

"No faster," I say. "No closer...Not schmart...."

"Speed is safety. That's the way you do it."

"No, that's the way we do it."

Clarence King

By the way, on the meta scale, the debate between uniformitarianism (that Nature functions as a kind of gigantic Swiss clock, governed by immutable natural laws, and overseen by the Creator and His Swiss Guards) and catastrophism (that sudden unpredictable violent changes shape the natural world, natural history being a parade of sore thumbs maimed in accident rather than a watch made in the Helvetic Confederation) was very much discussed and debated in the nineteenth century. Interestingly, one of the chief exponents of catastrophism was Clarence King. He may have been the chief lay exponent.

This is the same Clarence King who explored some corners of the Uintas in the 1860s as young leader of a government-sponsored survey. The same

Clarence King who has laid his tracks in this neck of the woods. The same Clarence King who put the Uintas on the map, who speculated much about their geology. The Clarence King who also wrote a book about climbing mountains in California, *Mountaineering in the Sierra Nevada*.

This was the same Clarence King who glittered in social and political throne rooms all the way to the White House. The same one who was thought of as the best and brightest of his generation by many, including his homie, the habitually third-personed Henry Adams.

That would be the same individual who had lent his name to the two highest peaks in Utah, Kings and South Kings, not named for any pasty-faced monarch rewarded for being born in the a lucky place, but for Clarence King, a somewhat self-made man, a handsome man with fair hair and beard, the best handsome man nineteenth century America could make, who had espied these very rocky Uinta heights and sought to explain their substance, their essence, how they were made, and how they were worn down by snow and ice.

This same Clarence King led a secret life. Later in his career, he married a darker-skinned woman, Ada Simpson, who may have been born into bondage, and had several children with her living in Brooklyn, New York, after he had done all this and all of that. Neither side knew of the other. The same Clarence King, mingling with Presidents and American Aristocracy, pretended to be a Pullman porter working on the railroad. (Working on the railroad explained his long absences.) Despite the lightness of his skin, he claimed to be a black man, and specifically of West-African descent. Moving in highest society and running a secret life. Dude had some moxie, Shirley.

Clarence King supported catastrophism because it lurked within him. Because any time it could burst upon him and reveal that which he was able to keep secret.

Because an edge is only an edge with the dizzy drops. Because you get up and down such an edge and you may want more of it, despite yourself, because of yourself.

If the world didn't know of his Brooklyn family, his Brooklyn family also did not know the figure he cut in the gilded world.

He died broke and consumptive in Tucson, Arizona, all alone. On his death bed he wrote Ada to tell her the truth.

(Some of this is based on Martha A. Sandweiss's *Passing Strange: A Gilded Age Tale of Love and Deception Across the Color Line.*)

In my experience, Kings and South Kings are two peaks which are frequently by no means visible because of the micro-scale catastrophism just then winding up to wallop the heights. No can see, Kings Peak, nor South Kings neither, Clarence, Clarence King.

And when the clouds lift, they will be covered with summer snow.

Dead Horse

We take a rest day after Wasatch. The following day we aim our steps toward Dead Horse Peak.

The sky plummets at the pass, but it falls noiselessly, so we just keep going.

We find ourselves on top of Dead Horse Peak in fog so thick that we see precisely nothing. Nothing. Just fog and mist, though, no lighting. The air does not move. It's foggy enough to seriously disorient a pilgrim.

We're only sure we've reached the top by abject triangulation. The lack of lightning is a good thing and makes up for seeing nothing. The day before yesterday's lightning show was good enough to last for a while.

It's an eerie, otherworldly scene up here.

The ridge was a schisty cakewalk, too, dirty black and brown with a few boulders sticking up: chortens or Moai. We'll get down it by following our divots in the rocky scruff and stay on-line. You just never know how a peak will turn out. This one just rolled over for us like a horse you pulled the saddle from.

Hours later, when the clouds burn off, we actually find the eponymous dead horse, or at least a dead horse, laid out in red-ocher boulders beneath the pass. It's a bit hard to figure. The dead horse we find, while not exactly fresh, doesn't look as old as a dead horse would have to have been to be the dead horse for whom the pass and peak are named. That must have been an older dead horse, another dead horse, but this one is dead, surely, and that one was dead, too, so maybe this is just a bad place to be if you're a horse. The entire West Fork trail is enough to kill a horse, we agree. Any horse. A good horse or a bad horse. A horse in the fog or in sunshine.

The bad weather on top and afternoon clearing we rue. It doesn't seem right that we walked all the way up there and saw nothing, but down here we see everything, even a dead horse.

The sun is just beaming down, mocking us. Maybe we should have just stayed down here. No, Dead Horse is on the list now, view or no view. Dead horse or no dead horse. We talk big for tomorrow.

In our morning puffery we have our eyes on Yard Peak, an imposing little flat-topped number on the west side of the West Fork. As we walk, we find we are really too worn out to give it much of a try.

Yard Peak is no three-hour tour. We walk up to a pass and dawdle around.

We haven't seen anyone for days, only dead horses. Whom do we run into on the pass? Three kids from a NOLS (National Outdoor Leadership School) group or one of those Hoods in the Woods wilderness-therapy outfits, two guys and a girl. We don't ask. Just after we exchange greetings, they ask us if we have any extra food. No questions about our itinerary or what it's like to nearly get fried. The girl is certainly better looking than Alpenglow, so despite the oddness of the request, we dig out some cookies, apples, a candy bar and hand them over. The kids simply wolf the food down. It's all gone in ten seconds, seeds and all. I've never seen American kids eat with that intensity. They give us looks of utter gratitude as we dig another Little Debbie out.

They've probably been living on one packet of oatmeal and one packet of delicious ramen per day for weeks. They aren't in the Uintas for fun and adventure, but rather for some type of treatment. Punishment as treatment. It's definitely Hoods in the Woods. And their parents had probably paid a pretty penny for the course, and it is probably because they're such rotten, materialistic parents who chose to live in Vermillion Ledges, California, in the first place.

What is the worth of that sort of treatment? Gosh, if it were me, when I got back to civilization, I'd sample a number of pizzas and indulge every potion I could. Just saying. Deprivation leads to binging, at least that's my experience. Rebellion exists for a reason, usually. They are decent kids, too. A few weeks out strips us of our pretentions. I'm thinking I wouldn't want them around for dinner.

Scrambling High Unita Peaks

And why take all the fun out of the wilderness anyway? The other thing I would take away from such treatment would be the strongest desire never to go back into the mountains, which is likewise wrong.

In truth, Alpenglow and I get so far out there for these weeks that the reentry is challenging. We could get our hands around the concept of scrambling peaks like there was no tomorrow. It was only a question of when and how many. But what's next?

Then there was real life. Real life didn't seem to be worth the trouble. Nowhere could one duplicate the strong lasting jollies, the serrated thrills of being all the way out there and somehow finding a misty steep way to get back. No, it was always better to be high up there than low down here. It could get you down.

Rosy Talus

The great obvious changes in the rocky crust were referred to a few processes: the subaerial decay of continents, delivery of land-detritus by streams into the sea, the spreading out of these comminuted materials upon a pelagic floor, the spreading out of these by which oceanic beds were lifted into subsequent land masses.

—Clarence King, 1877

These days, in high season, the Henry's Fork trail is thronged with pilgrims. Thronged! Refugees from Metro Utah, joined by faith or neighborhood, acting as their own celestial Sherpa,

89

they can be seen carrying (and dragging) their bulging fardels toward the holy heights. These ill-equipped pilgrims undertake the arduous journey up Utah's roof as a religious rite. For the feat, and for the feet of many it is a Via Dolorosa rather than a Way of Joyful Feelings.

And verily they will often find the main message in the heart of the Uintas: *Never Again. Never again shall ye trudge these rock-rich ridges. Never again shall ye walk through the valley of the shadows. Never again shall ye carry your belongings on your back and sleep upon the ground. Never again shall ye swat an unheavenly host of mosquitos. Never again shall ye walk so far to be closer to heaven, to look down upon the world.*

One call, Doll, that's all.

No mas, por favor.

At the same time, there are other groups of better-equipped gangs out for the high point, with a bit more experience in their rucksacks.

The second and third highest of Utah peaks, South Kings and Gilbert, are accessible from Henry's Fork, though both are usually ignored. The fourth highest, Mt. Emmons, can be observed from Gunsight Pass. Groups tend to make attempts exclusively on Kings.

Why here?

Because the Henry's Fork trail offers the shortest and most direct route to Kings Peak, Utah's most lofty protuberance and highest point.

Kings Peak throws up neither glacier nor cliff. There's a good trail nearly the whole way. Although a round trip ticket costs thirty miles, and there are some gruesome rocky up-hills, such a tariff separates much wheat from chaff. Weather and personal will are the chief limiting factors.

RED STONE HEART

Most pilgrims return with no worse hurts than sore muscles, raw shoulders and few blisters. Three long days usually suffice, with no time for fun. No fun, which is, for many, perhaps the point of this high point.

A better journey can be much longer or much shorter.

Perhaps also as a side attraction, Henry's Fork is good place to find a pinch of alpine splendor, some rocky chortens and the Truth. For The Truth can be found there: lowland rocky miles of it, high scalloped crumbly ridges of it. The way it lingers like a haiku or a psalm on the edges of a stream, and the prophet light at sunset.

A visit away from July and August can bring solitude and benefits. In the snowy seasons, it is a fine place to ski but let's not go there.

All have a right to try for Kings, and many do. Aside from the worry of weather, the route if dry offers only one complication. The normal way via Gunsight Pass goes out of its way to add a few miles in the interest of safety and pack animals, heads climbers' left in a big way, drops down into Painter Basin, then doglegs and doubles back on itself to a make a mule track to Anderson Pass and the top. From Gunsight, there is a scrambler's shortcut route that eschews the drop, a somewhat exposed traverse of slope and talus.

For would-be summiteers there is also a trail-less shortcut, breathtakingly obvious, that will lead from the upper Henry's Fork right on up to Anderson's and Kings. It is easy to see, and easy to see that it will be a slippery slope, a schisty, loose and rotten way. In other words, a pretty standard Uinta slog. Given its location, clearly not a good place to be with pilgrims poised above and below. Today this gully even has a name: the Toilet Bowl, which is grossly unfair to toilets.

This shortcut, the Toilet Bowl, features awful footing throughout. This is nothing unusual in the Uintas, but few of today's Kings Peak neophytes will have experience with the many schists of Sisyphus, the hard-won knowledge of the trademark Uinta slippery talus slope: dangerous for the way up, beckoning and dangerous for the way down.

The spooky yet desirable combination, though, of directness and loose, bad rock makes me believe that it will not be lightning but rather a heap of Big Rollers in the Toilet Bowl that will account for Kings injury reports, particularly when six or eight groups are in there, knocking rocks down on the others. Call it bowling in the bowels of the Uintas.

This is how things stand in the present day. In past epochs, things were different.

1987. We are driving. Larry Darkness, Mark Alpenglow and me. We are driving in a large powder-blue Oldsmobile Delta 88 diesel, my car, formerly my mother's (Sister Dona). It is late September and we are alone on the red dirt roads. We drive out of Mountain View, Wyoming, well stocked and ready.

We are listening to a cassette tape by New Order called *Low Life*. We like the way the pale and morbid Brits sing their songs and strum their guitars, the way the mix puts the bass to the front, and we especially like the nihilism. We are swilling Schmidt's, the one with the cutthroats on the cans. We are young and free. We are morbid and pale if sunburned. We are playing our four-string basses along with it, the best we can. We also like "Jacques the Monkey" and "Domestic Éclair."

Alpenglow and I are going out to lunch. We'll be away from the office for a few weeks. Please leave a number if you happen to call. We are out to affirm life. In doing so, we embrace a fashionable nihilism. Light and dark clash together in key like bass and guitar. And keyboards and nihilism. And A minor and D major seventh. And youth in these cold, old hills. These cold, red hills.

In real life I am living in a former gas station in Hoboken, New Jersey, the Garden State, where my pastimes include indulging low life and playing some different roles to get along. I have driven the big beautiful Oldsmobile across this great country from the East, and in a few weeks, I will drive it back, detouring through Canada. I do this to try to maintain my sanity. It's a great country, too, Canada.

"What are you running from, son?"

"Nothing, actually. I'm running to."

"You sure?"

Larry Darkness and Mark Alpenglow are both actually from New York State, hailing from Ithaca and Buffalo respectively. Will they ever return to their Blessed Isles? To the snow shadow of Erie, to the Finger Lakes? Why would they? Who can say?

We are going into the high country, the backcountry, to enjoy the alpine splendor and the sharp edge. The three of us vow to try anything and never fail, never turn back. That is our mission and our mission statement. You got a problem with that?

We love the trees. We salute the trees. These are western trees, western American trees, planted by no one, heard to fall by no one, of economic benefit to no one. When we stop to piss, we may embrace them. We embrace also the big beautiful powder-blue Oldsmobile that bears us along. To start her up requires removing the air filter cover, putting a screwdriver in the carburetor gate to keep it open, and spraying starting fluid in, then turning the key. It works nearly every time and then the Delta 88 is good all day.

It is late September. Winter comes early to the high country. Someday I hope to figure all this out. For now, though, it is enough to roar up the red dirt road toward the mountains. We roar for there is a hole in the tail-pipe muffler assembly. We hail the lodgepole pines. We don't forget the Motor City. We salute the arching sky, streaked with high cirrus, saluting our veterans and love vigilantes. We play the tape again. It's the middle of the week and the piedmont is empty of people. We feel lucky. We are lucky. The rest of the world is working. For what, we have to ask, for what?

"For what?"

"For what?"

"For what?"

No answer. We are working, too. Working on getting as far out as we can.

We arrive at the Henry's Fork trailhead toward evening, saddle up and walk until we can see no more and bivouac on the trailside. The next day we walk far up into the basin. At the last straggly trees, we pitch our tents, beneath the red-runneled western slopes of Gilbert Peak.

RED STONE HEART

On the summit day, with clouds lowering, we find that the Toilet Bowl is unsullied, still clean and fresh. There's hardly even a goat path up its slipshod length. It's an early-morning slippery slide, slanting the opposite way from up. From the top of it, we cross the flat toward Anderson Pass, and clamber up the Death Platters to the top of the state. Yet again we stand the highest people in Utah.

Indeed, because the weather is dismal and threatening, we feel certain we are the highest by a large margin. Nobody else is on top of high peaks today, both because it's late September, and because all the other peaks are socked in. How dismal? How threatening?

Miraculously, only Kings remains aloof, an island above the fray. How is it that everywhere else is socked in? It's raining and probably snowing over there, and there, and there. There's a kind of dome, a bubble, above us, and all around us the soup. Here sort of sunshine. And quiet, so far. It's a miracle, surely. We give thanks and praise.

Beneath the dusky clouds, the lower-down view presents itself, large and sweeping. The Mellowstone drainage curves away to the south, dotted here and there with clumps of yellow-gold aspen, one luxurious sweep of landscape, with enough length to be truly wild in its plenty. On the other side, Painter Basin is a marvel of golden bogs, russet this-and-that and yellar willer. Completing the circle, Henry's Fork stretches green and red and spruce-blue and fine.

Looking through our weather window, it must be said that September is the best time to be above ten thousand feet in the high country of the American West. There is the color of the vegetation, soon to be de-leafed, but held now in splendid culmination. The streams are clear, mirroring afternoons golden and lightly blazing, to say nothing of the bracing nights, long but not overly so, just about right. There fly no bugs nor mill no other pilgrims. The odious sheep and tender cattle have lifted tail for the lowlands. You might hear the lovelorn whistle of elk or coyotes clowning of an afternoon.

Okay, but the only drawback to September is the threat of weather, bad weather, nearly always rain then shortly snow, heralded by the warm west breeze that will shift to the cold icy moist of the north. Snow is good but obliterates the trails, makes the rocky passages gravy-slick and dangerous, and tends to make all the things it touches wet and, by degrees, coldly shivering.

As I say, it's raining and probably snowing nearly everywhere else. Emmons, Lovenia, Wasatch, Tokewanna, Explorer, even nearby Gilbert--all obscured, getting plastered.

We point to our general uprightness as reason for being dry, we lucky few.

Larry busies himself looking at the map, again. Alpenglow is reciting his collection of Uinta peaks. He can't see them, any of them, but he is declaiming his list from the last two summers. He names one short of a dozen. He names them again and then again.

It brings up a problem we need to discuss. Alpenglow claims that his two ascents of Ostler Peak count as two peaks, and we say that they do not, that a peak is a peak and an ascent is an ascent. The Nordwand and the Hourglass routes are two ascents of one peak.

"Alpenglow, I was in your presence both times," I expand. "The one and then the other. They were grand, but two is one, son."

"No. Two is two!" he demands.

"No, actually not."

"Two is one, not two," says Larry. "No matter all the talking that you do."

"Two is one, not two."

"Two is one, not two."

"Two is two and hell with you," Alpenglow decides.

On the other hand, our calculus for the next move is simple and we find quick agreement. It is still fairly early, well before noon, even though, to be frank, the heavens have grown extremely dark and threatening. Our mojo will get us through. It is not every day that one has an actual chance to do a twofer of the tops.

Might as well try for South Kings Peak, we agree. It's just a mile south along the ridge, only forty feet shorter than Kings. This will make our day complete. We'll be there in twenty minutes. We race.

(It will prove to be one of the best decisions I will ever make. A lot of people manage to climb Kings Peak. A lot of people never ascend South Kings. Why would they? Because seen from the west, or south, South Kings looks higher and is surely more impressive, would be one strongly compelling reason. The top is the top, and South is just table scraps, second fiddle, number two. Probably only one percent ever goes for number two.)

As we find ourselves there, we know we are among the elect. We feel that our electness ought to be celebrated. But at the South Kings summit graupel bounces on the already-rain-slick rocks. We observe that the Lovenia cloud is now our cloud. We note that the Emmons cloud is now also our cloud. That of Gilbert is approaching. We feel this is not an entirely optimistic thing.

Sudden loud noises can be heard. The graupel plummets earthward and gathers in slick white clumps. Rabbit turds. It's time to skidaddle from SoKings.

Given that Kings can no longer be seen, we know that going back that way is out of the question. We have had experience with this kind of weather. We see this as quite a bit like those other times, which we do not hanker to relive. We decide to drop directly into Painter Basin, go straight east down the slag heap, and get down low as quickly as possible. We have no other good options.

The rumbling of nearby cloud-to-cloud electrical exchange causes us to move with strong intention in our downward sashay over the wet and rolly rosy talus.

A thousand vertical feet lower, our good luck with the weather holds, mostly. The graupel gives way to light drizzle as our own personal cloud lifts. Everywhere else is lost in soup. No sunshine here, but neither blizzard nor lightning — that's over there, there and there. It's a miracle, surely.

Larry Darkness, Mark Alpenglow and I feel like three kings and mention it often. Three Kings of Kings and South Kings. We kings. We regal. We congratulate ourselves for our regal accomplishments, our kingly deeds. It's almost safe enough for a rest stop.

RED STONE HEART

All these processes are held to have been
more rapid in the past than now. Suddenness,
world-wide destructiveness, are characteristic
of geological changes... Periods of calm, like
the present, suddenly terminated by brief
catastrophic epochs, form the groundwork of
this school.

—Clarence King, 1877

Mark Alpenglow likes a little show. He enjoys noise as well as drama. Even though he is working on a Master's in wildlife biology, he doesn't always maintain a strict scientific detachment toward all living things. He plays favorites. He anthropomorphizes at times. He's not above encouraging natural processes.

He specializes in small and medium-sized mammals, especially members of the weasel family, but expresses nothing but contempt for squirrels: too noisy, too territorial, too freaking close, too damned early, and even less for hapless chipmunks, poor striped bastards. Also, he casts a dark eye and some harsh words toward most songbirds, and all deer, hares and rabbits. They can ruin his quietude, his wilderness experience.

Yet 'Glow is the master of the spot-the-wildlife photograph. He snaps slides of them using Kodachrome. He has racks and racks: nearly always some vast swath of vegetation with some tiny spot of animal in it: perhaps a black bear or that's-got-to-be-a grizzly, or a pine marten or marmot, or an elk or mountain goat. You usually have to squint to see them.

99

Scrambling High Unita Peaks

To be entirely honest, they do not make for the most stimulating slide show. True, whenever he gets close enough to make the shots really count, he'll burn many frames in capturing nature's faunal grandeur, but many of his slide shows are predominantly of the spot-the-wildlife stripe, as exciting as math class, as boring as the Henry's Fork trail.

I cannot and do not endorse the practice of rolling rocks (trundling) down mountainsides for fun and pleasure. It is always dangerous. It can be deadly. It causes erosion. It interferes with natural processes, making a type of ersatz catastrophism. And it is also wrong in half a dozen other ways. Wrong! It's even illegal in places. Illegal!

Even when you are certain you are alone, as we are, it is wrong to trundle. Bad! Wrong!

By 1987, I have already become a reformed trundler, a rock roller in recovery. One who once rolled but does so no longer. One who has learned the many steps to repentance. One who lives with a talus of regret.

Mark Alpenglow has not reached that point yet. Somewhere in the rosy talus, making our retreat from the socked-in summit of South Kings, he comes upon a very large rock, a chunk of rufous quartzite that seems more than willing to roll, with just a touch, a gentle touch, a ptarmigan's peck on the side of it. He touches it. He rolls it. Once rolled, this rock dislodges another and yet another. Cackling with delight, enjoying the bouquet of busted rock, the spicy smell, the rumbles both deep and clanging,

he urges more rocks along. Many others. He does a workout with them. He gets physical. There rolls a regular rock barrage.

Much of the range reposes in this manner: uniformitarianism waiting for catastrophe.

Oh dear. Darkness and I watch warily. We do not participate. We touch not the rocks to roll. Soon we see how the rockslide's fling and flang down the slope boasts has an unintended consequence: it has startled a herd of elk down below in Painter Basin. We see them running away.

We know how the elk like to while away their afternoons in the mini-meadows right at the base of the peaks, because we have spied them doing so. This is probably because the air is fresh and clean, the occasional breeze keeps the bugs at bay, tasty late-season streams still flow among the hummocks and bedrock pools, proximity to escape terrain allows the wooly beasts a chance to relax and masticate tender forbs, grass and sedges, and maybe because the elk like to be up high to enjoy the view.

If they do not move, we do not see them.

Spotting the elk herd, 35mm camera in hand, Mark Alpenglow takes off romping down the talus, through a wake in the rock his recent handiwork has wrought, hoping to snap a treasure trove of spot-the-wildlife photographs of the magnificent roving wapiti of Painter Basin. In a few moments he is far down the slope.

Once the rock dust has settled, Larry D. and I consider our options. The weather is holding, not great, just drizzle but not blizzard either. To follow Alpenglow's tracks and drop down into the basin would exact a great deal of huffing and puffing to regain Gunsight Pass — a long and unnecessary detour that violates the first rule of mountaineering: never lose elevation unnecessarily. No, we will stay level with this level. We will traverse. We will test the edges of our Italian leather boots. We will undertake a long, level and gruesome traverse over rose-colored, ankle-testing talus from this point to the pass. We'll slip and slide, for there is a lot of shiftiness in the stone, but we will have no cliffs to skirt or climb. We'll hope the weather holds. We'll try to get ourselves safely back to camp before dark or storm where we'll wait for Alpenglow and hope he is not lost or too far behind.

RED STONE HEART

Larry Darkness and I discuss our options back at high camp. We cook dinner and save a large portion for Alpenglow, kept in a pot in his tent on his sleeping pad and wrapped in his spare sweater, one he might like to have just now. We save it for him, should he return.

Camped at the highest trees in the canyon, we have very fine seats for the sunset spectacle: glowing red terraces wet with rain, skying-anvil clouds of salmon and yellow, Durga light in the willow stands and meadows, an occasional whang of rock fall. It is good to prepare to sleep way up in some canyon. We cannot sleep, of course, until our buddy returns. Nor can we go out and find him. There is way too much ground to cover. If we have to search, we'll start at first light.

A night out is never out of the question. Let's just say that we know he has a lighter and matches which can make a night out unpleasant but bearable and survivable, if one can drop down to trees. In late September at 12,000 feet, the temperature will probably be in the 12-18 degree range. Cold, certainly, but not that cold. Well…there will be no rain. In fact, the clouds lift, presenting a yellow-orange sunset courtesy valance.

In the dark, we take turns shining our lights around and hollering. Only stars not blocked by clouds. It's chilly. We shout and call, "Eh-dee."

After much time he shows up, out of the darkness. He's got great photos of the elk, of course, can't wait to get them developed. He did end up a canyon over from where he thought he should and was lost, really lost. Climbed a ridge to figure out where he was. Wasn't exactly sure where he was. Crossed a basin, climbed another ridge. Crossed some sickening boulder fields. Made Gunsight, well, made Gunsight somewhere after dark. Or course he had a flashlight, but the batteries were dying. Thought he heard us from way back up there and was glad to hear us.

"Here, Alpenglow, we saved you some glop." We accompany him to his tent with the goodies. "Lipton noodles with onion and Brother Beef."

"Thanks, Man. It's good to see you guys... Good to see anyone out here."

He sits down, his boots sticking out the tent door. He does not hesitate to eat it.

"We were a bit worried at the end," I say as we watch him devour.

"It's getting a little cold tonight," adds Larry.

"Not necessarily for your sake, of course, but because we didn't want to have to go out and look for you," I say.

"Man, this is good," Alpenglow says.

"No, it would not have been good," Larry says. "To go out, not good."

Not good," I say. "Hello darkness, your old friend..."

"No, that is not good," Alpenglow says, "This is good."

"Is it good?"

"It is good," he says.

"Good, or very good?"

"Very good or very, very good?"

"YES, IT IS VERY GOOD. IT IS VERY, VERY GOOD."

"Goooooooood," says Larry. "Here is also

good. No danger. Gooood. We warm in tents. Warm is good. Tents good. Lipton is good. All is good. No walking around in the dark…That's not good."

Alpenglow nods his head and grunts. "Good, veddy good."

He then falls asleep midsentence, passing out on top of his sleeping bag, with his boots still on. We pluck the pot out and toss it some distance from camp in case of marmots or bears. He can clean it in the morning. He's already sawing branches.

"Two is one not two."

"Two is one not two."

We zip his up and return to our own tents.

We take our time in walking out the Henry's Fork. We spread it out over an entire day's work.

We have time. We are in our mid-twenties and none of us has a regular job, though we do have degrees. Sometimes Larry paints houses. Often he does not paint houses. Me, I read legal briefs in New York City. I work in the World Trade Center and at 60 Wall St. I'm a temp. Here in the Uintas, I am young and free, not a temp.

Mark will continue graduate school in a couple of weeks. He has a Logan routine that works for him. Study all week between labs and take field trips. Hit the White Owl on Friday night, climb five thousand vertical feet on Saturday, usually Logan Peak, usually walking from the house he shares with a couple of other wildlife-bio dirtbags. Sunday means a twelve pack and football. He prefers Old Milwaukee because it is cheap and provides the lightest hangover. He's tried all the brands to test his hypothesis, his scientific method. Being from Buffalo, he's a Bills fan, an ardent Bills fan, and as such, he knows the value of suffering. He will know the value of much more.

Real life? Walking at a leisurely pace out of the mountains on a September day is as real as it gets, as real as it needs to get.

The ever-present of the walk about, the dreams of other trips and places, all steps along the road. It feels like it'll last forever and you still want more.

Incidentally, the decision to bag South Kings will prove unusually prescient and wise, for myself, one so young and not given to excessive reflection or planning. Years later, when Tee Trundler, Sean McHelen and I dedicate ourselves to rounding out the Notorious Nine, they will both be stymied and saddened by a lack of South Kings on their list. Without being asked I will gladly mention that it is in my collection already, in the safe, embossed on fine Corinthian leather. Indeed, one by one the Uinta giants will fall for us but not South Kings for them.

Trundler will undertake a grotesque one-day ascent of Kings with some friends, skiing all the way to the top and back in a twenty-two hour suffer-fest that covers thirty-six miles and begins and ends in the darkness, a journey he says, "Taught me several things about what was possible…and also about the possibilities of pain."

Not surprisingly, Tee doesn't express much interest in returning to Kings, and the easiest route to South Kings is over Kings, and this lack continues to cause him sorrow and unease. Likewise, Larissa McHelen will stand atop Kings with her tall little man, Sean, but she and he have never stood on the South one. If I get my nine, they will be left with eight, which is great.

Out Watching Birds

*There are two populations of Tundra
Swans in North America-one in the east and
one in the west... The western population
breeds on the west coast of Alaska and winters
on the Pacific Coast and in the Central Valley of
California. In Utah, the calls of wild swans can
be heard echoing across marshes during spring,
fall and winter. Western populations arrive in
the Great Salt Lake area in late October and
begin departing by early December en route to
their wintering grounds.*

— *Tundra Swan,*
Utah Division of
Wildlife Resources
Wildlife Notebook Series
No. 20

RED STONE HEART

On the day after Thanksgiving, 1988, Mark Alpenglow and a fellow graduate student and friend, Paul Richie, launch a homemade boat into a fresh-water arm of the Great Salt Lake to look at birds. By late November, much of the annual migration of many species of birds would be largely over, especially birds of the smaller stripe. Some birds would linger for a few weeks, and some birds were just coming in for the season. The good thing, at least according to Alpenglow, was that most of the small, annoying birds would be gone.

Tundra swans, a striking, large and highly musical bird were likely to be around, passing thru. Bald eagles, too, who wintered in the area, would be setting up shop. Bald eagles were a cinch to spot: striking, majestic, and imbued with certain national significance. Few sights are as moving to most bird-lovers as the tundra swan or the bald eagle flying against a white-washed, overcast late-fall sky. In such conditions the creatures are pure movement, kinesthetic perfection expressed in motion certain to make those of us tethered to earth verdant with envy.

When the Mother Goddess created these two, She surely earned Her rest days.

A homemade boat, speaking generally, might be a good idea as a hobby project for well-seasoned shipwrights. Boats are best which do not leak, and boats which move keeling straight and easily, are also superior to those which clunk, founder or track like the snake rather than the falcon. On the other hand, a pre-owned canoe or river-worn inflatable might be available from collegiate outdoor programs, including the one at Utah State University, which Mark Alpenglow and Paul Richie were then attending, but they might be expensive.

What better use could be made of a weekend between football games or during bad ones than tinkering on a homemade boat? The Autumns of Logan, Utah, are often breathtakingly beautiful, before the snow and temperature inversions set in.

The stark gray mountains of the Bear River Range, which surmount the valley's east side, do so in shapely, various and darned pretty ways: here a forest of mountain mahogany, there some north-facing spruce dens, southward tasteful limestone gendarmes and cliffs. To say nothing of the aspiring Wellsville Mountains across the way, steep, simply serrated and undeniably mountains.

A boat like most tools is not something one should like to share. It should be the prerogative of the owner and all that bestows. Most graduate students might have a hard time scraping together enough hundreds to buy a shiny new canoe, built on an aluminum frame, and sided with Royalex or Kevlar. That tariff would be uncomfortably close to a quarter's tuition.

Wood floats. Get enough of it together and you can float a menagerie. Wood bends when soaked in water. Wood is widely available in the wild, at lumber stores, in dumpsters, in the neighbor's backyard, and cast off in a hundred places. One-by planks, then, are not that hard to find. And as for design, why not improvise? What doesn't work can be fixed with nails and caulk and glue.

In the carport of a rented rambler on "The Island" in Logan, Utah, a boat, a vessel, begins to take shape. Yea, verily the gods of the wine-dark sea have been speaking to all who lend a hand. It takes shape, girth, displacement. It has bow and stern and draft and beam.

November, November. What more prefect hours can be found than those few brilliant, shining, sunlight on gold and freshly-white slopes?

What's up with migrating birds? What makes them do so much? Moving from here to there? What place is home, summer or winter? The tundra swan covers 4000 kilometers twice a year.

Who said this is a good idea?

The migration of certain birds violates every law known to physics. The migration of certain birds violates every law of utility. The tundra swan covers 4000 kilometers twice a year.

From here to the Island Market is a distance that can be measured in numbered steps. Those are the numbered steps to procure the twelve pack.

The tundra swans do what they do. They do what they do. Yet is it not way more than probable that they do not need to do what they do?

They do what they do.

They do not need to do what they do? Maybe they do?

They do what they need to do.

Paul and Mark paddle out onto the lake. They paddle and paddle. The bay is calm and large.

Many days in November are marked by

gold, white and blue. The colors of the tundra swan. The color of the golden eagle. The color of untracked poofder. The colors of the morning breeze on Old Main Hill. The color of the Great Salt Lake at sunset. The color of all that is good on the land.

Out on the lake, with the view of the Wasatch Wall newly-dusted, Mark and Paul, in their homemade boat, in search of *Cygnus columbianus,* in search of the Columbian swan, the Tundra Swan, a skinny girl that thinks you're grand, they paddle the wine-dark wind-kissed freshwater arm of a great dead sea.

All of the Wasatch waters end up here and much of the West End and North Slope waters of the Uintas, too. The Uinta waters run east and north, downhill but not to the ocean.

It's a Great Basin, a Great Salt Lake, and a great homemade boat.

From the northwest comes a storm cloud, gossamer and quiet, in the distance. White gray against gold and blue. Gold of bobbing wood. Blue of the dead sea water, curving like a lover's kiss, like the wings of a tundra swan, like the hope of a promise, like the censors of the church.

Gold, white and gray blue. Then very dark gray blue.

Suddenly the waves are angry. Suddenly the waves bob the homemade boat. Suddenly the waves slap the homemade boat. Suddenly the waves want something gold for ransom. Suddenly the waves...

He remembers that there were two wet suits. He remembers that there were two wet suits. He remembers that of the two set suits one is worn by Paul Richie. Paul who is holding onto the gunnels of the boat. Suddenly he remembers that of the two wet suits he declined one to wear.

He said, "Why in God's Green Acres would I want to wear a wet suit, Paul? We're not going scuba diving."

The waves. That northwest curving cloud, all encompassing. What was calm is no longer calm. It is jumping.

What it means to look up the skirt of the pines at night in the high mountains.

What it means to climb the loose slopes in the high mountains.

What it means to get OUT THERE.

The White Owl.
The Great Salt Lake.
The golden foothills of Farmington.

The scientific method must concern itself with what can be demonstrated as observed. As observed, noted, shown. Speculation overthrown.

The boat flips, swamps. Mark Alpenglow and Paul Richie go for a swim, a swim a long way from shore. Now they are holding onto the boat and kicking.

There is no way to right the homemade boat. The boat that was homemade in the carport on the Island in Logan, Utah. The boat that bobs but that is way too heavy to right. It is way too heavy to right. Heavy it is, it cannot be righted. Not righted it bobs. It bobs as one holds on to it. Holding on to it, one will not go down.

Scrambling High Unita Peaks

Logan Peak cannot be seen from the bay. Ben Lomond is on display and other summits run all the way down the Wasatch Wall to Lone Peak. Logan Peak is large and grand, yet its elevation is 9,741 feet. To reach its summit by foot from the city of Logan involves starting on the shoreline of Lake Bonneville, about forty-four hundred feet. Thus, the route from town climbs a vertical mile. Such a slog will let you know you are alive.

He had climbed it over thirty times. Nothing he could do could make it ten thousand feet high.

In November, persistent atmospheric cold causes the temperature of the waters to gradually decline, to decline to match the cold of earth, earth always being just a bit colder.

Fifteen minutes in cold water is not good. Thirty minutes in cold water is not good. One will feel the chill of November. One will feel the chill, the keel.

An hour in cold water, kicking toward shore is not good for the general physiology. The hamstrings tighten. The legs become hurting. Hurting, the legs become stiff. The hamstrings inflame. Stuck at ninety degrees. Bent, tight.

The legs hurt and hurt and hurt and hurt and hurt and hurt and hurt and hurt and hurt and hurt and hurt and hurt and hurt and hurt and hurt. And then the legs no longer hurt. And when they do no longer hurt the trouble begins.

The smell of nutmeg and patchouli. The arms. The hands at the end of the arms. The hands at the end of the arms are no longer useful. They are useless, chunks of wood.

The lungs. The lungs are always important, suddenly more so. The vessels and sacs constrict as though one had just had a killer deep hit of some fine Columbian. *Cygnus columbianus.*

Hands like chunks of wood.

Distant golden, blue mountains, richly white with recent snow. A great homemade boat.

"I came into the water because of the strong north-northwest breeze, that was the one that sent me into the water.

Mother, I have made a mistake.

Mother, will you help me?

Mother, you are already gone?

Mother, why are you already gone?

M-M-Mother.

But I am not that breeze. And I am not that water. I am lungs.

I am lungs."

The lungs.

Tight as with the good herb. That which constricts the capillaries. That which pinches in aorta, and Hell, all the big vessels.

"I am in the water, blood thickening like paste. My blood. My tissues, like lab samples. Observe. Mother, I am dying. I am dying, but it is impossible for me to be."

The homemade boat bobs.

The wetsuit, no thanks.

Not in this way, sent off like a tundra swan.

Observe the waves are cruel, slap happy.

"The cold.
The cold.
The.
The.
The.
The.
Th.
Th.
Th.
T.
.
.
."

Paul Richie, in a super-human effort, has got the homemade boat to shore. Mark Aplenglow, his friend, his buddy, barely had held on, blue eyes glassy, whitish-lipped, porcelain blue-faced, crumpled at ninety degrees, cold as shoreline rocks, stiff as driftwood, gone as yesterday, young as April, innocent as the Blessed Virgin, well, there he is, with a bit of spittle running from his mouth, foamy spittle bubbling. D-D-D. M-M-M. Oh Jesus, this cannot be happening.

And there was nothing that young Paul Richie could do, there was nothing that young Paul could do but run, run, run, run, run, run, run, run, run to the nearest human habitation, pound on the door, just about as scary as an unbloody dude can be, and say, "Won't you pl-pl-pl-pl. Pl-please call 911, my friend n-needs help.

My friend is down on the jetty.
Laid out like Kennedy.

RED STONE HEART

My friend needs help.
Please call now.
Please call.
Now.

Terminus

The first hospital was only seven ambulance miles away, but way too much time had passed. Pulse, not really. Heartbeat, no. Body temperature, below 90.

They called for a helicopter transport. They called for helicopter transport, and on the day after Thanksgiving, 1998, Mark Alpenglow was being taken to a big-time hospital trauma center. This was not in the plan.

It is against protocol to bag a cold, dead, young person. The protocol is to warm the body first with a variety of machines. They can pump warm saline into the stomach, and gradually warm the core. They can loosen up the blood and run it through a machine that can bring the blood up to a temperature, and by degrees, this warmed blood can be passed through the mortal remains of a person, so that the tissues can revive, the brain re-boot, the heart even — with sufficient shock — can be made to beat again, and yea verily there are a lot of potions that can be applied to reinvigorate all of the good and serviceable organs. Although this is extremely unlikely, there are a few cases in which it has worked, a very few cases, nearly always with young people, in this case, they are obligated to give it a try. It's not likely here but there's protocol.

Despite much effort, there is no meaningful response. The next-of-kin is his brother who lives in Salt Lake City. The family resides near Buffalo, New York. Richard Boyer must say goodbye to his errant brother. He must call his family. He will stand alone.

He will stand alone and tell them it is okay to pull the plugs.

To pull the plugs because there is nothing else that can be done. Brain dead isn't funny anymore. Because everything that can be done has been done. Everything that could be done was done. Done, it was not enough.

It is over.

It is over.

Gold, blue and white and over.

I pictured a rainbow.

You held it in your hands.

The blessed Virgin.

His mother. All our mothers.

To lose one's son, to lose one's son, to lose one's son.

Children are supposed to outlive parents.

Scrambling High Unita Peaks

Children are supposed to outlive Siblings. Friends.
Lovers. Acquaintances. Partners.
    Abandonment of love. Love.

    Seven months later, at the summit of Lone
Peak we gather in ceremony, his friends, his brothers,
to return his remains to earth.
    We form a circle, try to mouth useless
words — how at least, we are all together — then open
the urn and slowly scatter dust and small shards of
bone still stained with his marrow.
    In the marrow runs blood of summer and
mountains and madness and clouds.
    Ashes is too vague a word. We hold Mark
in our hands, more intimate than lovers. We try to
make sense of the accident and how organs, flesh
and eyes — a body we had climbed beside and slept
beside — has become fine powder and aggregate, life
dough mixed with tears.
    And that which remains — the first dusting
of snow.
    Maybe there's a better place we go, but no
place could be finer than a mountain top, beneath
a tent of sky, where memories circle full-feathered.
    Yet this summit is a resting place found five
decades too soon.

RED STONE HEART

The Magnificent Uinta List
of
Dr. Mark Alpenglow
1980-1987

Ostler Peak (twice)
Bald Mountain (West)
Kletting Peak
A-1 Peak
LaMotte Peak
Beulah
Red Knob
Wasatch Peak
Dead Horse Peak
Kings Peak
South Kings Peak
North Cathedral (Mt. Alpenglow)

Granola Fuel

Scrambling High Unita Peaks

Part III
Schistosity

1990s

What distinguishes a mica schist from a gneiss is not the mineralogical composition, although gneiss is somewhat richer in feldspar, but the type of fracturing: gneiss breaks into coarser pieces and also breaks with difficulty into small cubes or thick slabs, whereas mica schist fractures easily and into thin units because of its greater schistosity.

— Annibale Mottana et al.
S&S Guide to Rocks and Minerals.

Scrambling High Unita Peaks

Heavy Weather

I did not deal with Alpenglow's death very well. It made me sad and gave me a reason for sadness. Sadness is jealous of its rivals. First sadness can leave a deep mark, a bergschrund for other sadness to slide into. At the same time, I carried around these memories of incredible affirmation, of how great it felt to be fully engaged in something all-encompassing, an effort to get as far out there as one could, to spend a lot of time on the sharp edge. And there was also the madcap humor and straight silliness of it, and him, and the things that we did.

I felt sad that those feelings of wild affirmation seemed to be gone, given what happened, and that made me sad, because I wanted to have that strong and wild affirmation back or have the possibility of it forward, but it was gone and would not come back.

I had been married only a few months when this sadness came to me, and I did not handle it well. I handled it with vices, which helped nothing and hurt more than it helped, and the only thing that any of this did was contribute to problems in and with a first marriage, and when it ended, prematurely, I did not know how to deal with that sadness either.

This may surprise the reader, but I've always been kind of a loner, not always through choice, and I don't mind socializing one bit so long as there's the possibility of drama and song, or if I can be the center of attention. When I found the Dead Babies it was great because there were always people to go out and do something with. I always liked to have friends. This was one of the problems with a divorce. I had a partner round-the-clock, but when it was over, I didn't.

An unsuccessful first marriage doesn't merit discussion here except insofar as I found a clear motive to rediscover the Uintas again, something that seemed solid enough to last and stay.

1992. Sometimes you have to go off by yourself to figure out how to get back into it.

This has been a dry year with an early spring. In June I decide to re-ascend Lamotte Peak for some wilderness therapy, to try to figure out which of my current pains is greater and try to leave it behind, under rocks. It should have been clear which is, and it is, but I have to go back to see if I can get started again. I don't tell anyone where I'm going. My parents are out-of-state on an LDS mission.

I walk up the Stillwater alone and make

camp on a shelf above the snowmelt-roaring river. In the morning, I leave a note in my tent in case I don't come back. Along the way I discover that it's harder to get up this hill than before, with Alpenglow. Or it seems harder. Maybe I just forgot how long it is. I try to think about Alpenglow, his absence but mainly I have a thousand pointless conversations with Norah going up the steep gravelly forest and onto the red-green melting summit ridge.

You don't deal with ghosts through will but rather through chance, and the whole day is overwhelmed by the closer heart trauma, more compelling of attention than memories of Alpenglow. Norah's treachery and my part in it is something I can get my hands on.

The memories of him are still here but fading, graying and growing like names on an aspen. None of the accident makes any more sense now than it had four years earlier. It was a foolish mistake that he made, and bad luck. We were reckless. He was especially reckless. The recklessness lit up the night like far-off lightning.

At the summit, in warm spring weather rather than a September blizzard, I see a parade of peaks, many we had climbed, standing like waves in a red rocky sea, but already receding, as in the rearview mirror. The same but different peaks on a different day: the last time I was here with him I saw nothing but snow and gales, heard nothing but the wind and several strokes of lighting that chased us off the summit and all the way across high meadows.

Grizzly Man says, "You climbed LaMotte twice? Sometimes you deserve the punishment that you get, son. You still have to a lot to learn."

I take a direct way south from the summit, down a mushy snow-choked gully. I then cross the upper basin, work my way down through forest and meadows and across glacially-polished rock ribs, and end up back at camp edgy but hopeful things will get better now, all that memory-talus is behind me now that I've made a long-day statement about it.

I use my in-case-I-don't-come-back note to start a fire.

As I'm tending it, a cow moose wanders into view. I stir the embers and she comes closer, just a cow moose, late in the day, but she stops no more than forty-five feet away. I don't move too much, to avoid startling her, but even when I do she just watches me. Eventually she hoofs a divot in the duff and beds down, still watching me with dark brown eyes. I move carefully, fiddling around with supper, soup to noodles to cocoa, and the moose stays nearby, big ears twitching at flies, watching. She doesn't leave until it's nearly dark, when she gets up and moves away, walking down the canyon.

Thus, in the end I discover why I climbed Lamotte again.

By the 1990s others have gotten tied down with jobs and kids or better choices, so Tee Trundler is my go-to guy when contemplating adventures. We talk about the next Wind Rivers trip on the phone or in Tee's map room. Regarding the big red range, we have our eyes on Tokewanna.

Although we live in different places, we try to ski together in season.

RED STONE HEART

Tee and I are both stylish and accomplished skiers. My style comes only through years of devoted service to the Mother Goddess of the Untracked Pooofer. Tee's more coordinated and athletic. We like to ski together and rip it up, occasionally on *piste* but usually off. We're still using Asolo and Fabiano leather boots and very long (205-210 cm) yet narrow skis. Voile 3 pin bindings. Though we have free heels, we seldom telemark. We do the Alta parallel. You got a problem with that?

Tee skis around. Heck, he'll tour with anybody. But when Still-Sort-Of-Young Kevin comes around, liking to ski together lends itself to the talk of peak bagging.

Sometimes less is more. Last November, needing to get our minds off our troubles, Tee and I went skiing at S & M, our gateway to the Uintas. It was just like old times, like college days, unattached times when we would ski all day for a couple dozen turns but relished the solitude. Just like old times except that there was only between one and three inches of snow anywhere.

I use the term skiing loosely. It was pre-early season. We spent the best part of the day out "skiing" on snow, gravel, brush, grasses, cow cabbage, macadam, duff, dirt, whatnot. The insufficient cover demanded our attention. But we swore to keep 'em on, though, no matter what.

All day long I wanted to tell him about how my marriage was falling apart, and how bad I felt about it, and how I had been betrayed by people I had trusted, and of course how it was all my fault, too, but instead we just skied and skied in expectant silence.

Finally, in the car at day's end I got all blubbery, weepy and blubbery. He said, "Yeah, I knew you had something on your mind..." When I told him about the you know, and all that, and he assessed it pretty well. "Sometimes people get past that, usually not. No, usually not... What do you want to happen?" I told him I wanted it to stop hurting so bad. And so we glided down Oakley canyon toward whatever would happen next.

Since it is to be the weekend when my soon-to-be-ex-wife is going to pick up her stuff from my house in Richmond, Utah, I conceive it a very good time to be away, to find some slippery slopes for distraction.

Tee cares, sure, up to a point, but caring about someone else's love mess is like asking someone else to always be the one to be driving or needing to borrow a tool or piece of equipment: there are limits to caring and limits to crossing over that line. Listening is good; silence works, too.

The Slopes of Tokewanna

The prudent man foreseeth the evil and hideth himself, but the simple pass on and are punished.

— Proverbs 11:13.

Tee Trundler and I pause at the edge of the last stunted trees, look up at the mist-shrouded rubble-rich way ahead and have a tense discussion. We cannot see much of the East Face. The weather is not looking good. No, it's looking bad and looking likely to get worse. At times such as these, discussions are a good idea. It's important to make a sober analysis of pros and cons. It's a bad strategy to force the issue, unwise to try something that one is hesitant about.

Invariably, though, denial can work its magic at such times, fogging up better judgment like dark clouds bearing snow and rain.

There are three clear elements of trouble in the air: moisture, a breeze from the west, and our general impetus of heading to a higher altitude. Our start had not been unduly late. We had left camp well before 6:30 a.m.

The discussion takes place at approximately 10:30 am Mountain Standard Time in June, 1992. We share our under-spoken thoughts.

Will the clouds lift?

Tee and I are aware that they will not.

Will it rain and hail and sleet and perhaps even snow?

It surely will.

Will the wind blow and shake our parkas?

That will also happen.

How long will it take to get up this large, rearing face of ruined pink rock?

It will take two hours, at least. It may well take longer.

Will this put us on top at a bad time?

Yes. This will. We may be on top at a stormy and tempestuous time. We should therefore turn around. Turn around, go back to camp, and spend the rest of the day fishing, safe in our wisdom.

Yes, this is what we should do.

The initial part of the discussion is based on intuition rather than words, based on the nose and the eyes. It is a discussion of grunts and postures, a Kabuki.

On the other hand, factors in favor of continuing can be reduced to one: at the edge of stunted trees we are in a place where we can stand on top of Tokewanna in a couple of hours. If we use Occam's razor to slice the issue to its simplest core, then there it is, and here we huddle.

We spend most of our lives in places where such a statement would be untrue. It is a rare and indeed a lovely thing to be this close to the top of Tokewanna, couple of hours away. A compelling thing. A deeply urgent thing. We are very close. It was not easy to get here. *Carpe Diem*, as they say. Seize the carp.

When, at last, one of us decides to speak, it's merely, "Well, what do you think?"

"Think? Me? Ummm."

"What do you think?"

"I think, duh."

"Duh?"

"Duh."

"Duh."

"Duh-mb?"

"Duh-mb…"

"What do I think?"

"Okay, we've been over that."

Perhaps we're not good communicators. But we know better. What are we going to say? We know the odds and we know the arguments. We know the way the air feels and what it means. We know that out on the open slopes we'll be out on the open slopes. We know that as we near the top we will be nearing the top, arms out to all the weathers. Likely is wishful thinking. The certainty we feel in our guts: the dreaded thunder snow.

We know the simple imperative of mush, doggies, mush, the complications of retreat.

This may sound a little macho, and in truth our chests tend toward the hirsute, but neither

Scrambling High Unita Peaks

Tee nor I are likely be mistaken for macho guys, introverted, okay, weird, for sure, but not macho, well, not really. It's not exactly the case of who will blink first. Either one of us could get cold feet and want out.

The chance for chickening keeps our partnership interesting. *Bawk. Bawk.* I've baled on Tee numerous times, and even if it infuriated him, and it did, he never mentions it, or nearly never. There have been numerous other times when together we have refused to ski a particular slope or climb a line because we thought better of it or couldn't do it. Generally speaking, we are actually fairly cautious.

A rational person would know what to do. The solution is eminently rational: We'll hurry.

Upward we rush on here-till-Sunday talus. Lo and behold, though, as we gain on the face, the weather begins to improve. The fog lifts. True, it's still a little breezy, but the views begin to open up.

I shift into low gear and consider the treacheries of my soon-to-be-ex-wife and my soon-to-be-ex-best-friend, and this makes me very angry, and anger at such times is unproductive. So, then I don't think anything much at all beyond must... push...on. Get...to...the...top. Mush... doggie...mush.

South of Tokewanna across the way is a shapely peak we denote Tokeanother because it's a spitting image, really, the obvious choice. Here's

Tokewanna and there's Tokeanother. Another Tokewanna. It's easier to say than Nothertoke. Would you care to try for Tokeanother, brother? Tokeanother, someday, Tote Goat?

Beyond Tokeanother, Wasatch looms and 'round the corner, Lovenia can't be seen for the lingering clouds. Below us, the deep trench of the West Fork stretches u-shaped in its majesty, and across the way, the stupendous east face of Beulah, the North Cathedral, and all the other craggy business of steep ridges, pinnacles, turrets, and rotten cliffs—in the thick of where the peaks have no names.

The angle lessens but the way stays meandering and shitty. Arriving at the shoulder beneath the false summit, we notice that the clearing weather has been a sucker hole.

To the west, and not terribly far away, it is easy to observe that a very large and very gray cloud bank has formed. It has formed most large and oh-so-gray, midnight gray not Armani gray. Death-or-glory gray. A dark and moisture-laden whammy is headed immediately our way. A wet kiss.

At times such as these, simple gawking is not helpful. It doesn't take long to assess the situation. Also, denial doesn't work nearly as well at 12,800 feet as it does lower down.

Worse, it's virtually impossible to turn around. What will turning around get you at this point? Not much and probably not much more safety. The sorrow of turning around this close, too, can be wincingly great, as bad as sticking your neck out. Occam's razor.

The snow starts at the false summit. Summer snow is seldom good. Its shadow companion is lightning. We sing the song. "July and August snow we know. We also know the thunder snow."

We reach the false summit. The top, at the end of this rocky plank is lost in the white swirling distance. It strikes me that this will be the time I'm going to die on a high ridge in the Uintas during a blizzard. This time.... Zeus-the-Thunderer has us in his sights.

Tee will also die. We will both die, and it will take a long time for people to find us.

Actually it won't take all that long, just a little fly over, since we'll be laid out for all to see, right on the ridge, Bullseye Ridge, but it will be hard to get the bodies down, our fine young bodies, dressed in party regalia, perhaps lightly drifted with snow, well, not that hard to retrieve, really, just pick a calm morning, take a helicopter ride, drop a couple of jumpers with body bags, load the litter, fasten it down, winch it up, repeat, and that some people will be sorry about this, one or two, well, maybe...but easy to find, more or less.

We hear the thunder, see the white flashes. The electrical display is big, to the west and approaching. Big, then bigger, then extremely big, warming up to ring our bells.

One thing about summits under conditions such as these: they aren't restful. We tag the summit just to tag it, and start right back down, feeling not triumphant just triumphantly vulnerable.

Two minutes later we're stumbling toward the false summit, down the rocky plank, beginning to smear with snow, fully exposed and holding no other choice in the world.

A really bad feeling comes upon the mountaineer in such circumstances if there is a noticeable, sudden change in wind direction or air temperature. For instance, a parka-shaking moist warm updraft is not a good thing. Neither is a powder-pushing super-cold downdraft. These are conditions that should cause much fear.

Tee and I feel these sensations at the shoulder. We feel other strong sensations as lightning splits the dove-toned sky—just—over—there. *WHOOOOOOSH.*

Shee, Shee, Crick. WABAM!

Many strong physiological phenomena are associated with sudden encounters with violent weather, and these can be intensified by trauma brought on by fear, as, for example, when bolts, many unchained bolts of lightning begin popping, crashing and also grounding on the west shoulder of Tokewanna at 1:43 p.m. on June 21, 1992, just a stone's toss from Tee Trundler and I. A bunch of bolts.

The reptilian part of the brain takes over, its very substance is adulterated with terror. The escape instinct kicks in. Shedding excess detail, one feels a very strong desire to LEAVE THIS PLACE NOW.

In such circumstances, verily, the feet seem to leave the earth.

I notice that my partner is sprinting toward Tokeanother, arms wind-milling, backpack straps flying, great gobs of gravel being torn from the snow-covered rosy earth. Trundler is fleet of foot but has never run faster.

Behind the scarecrow-partner, I find myself also running all-out toward the escape gully spied earlier in the day.

Scrambling High Unita Peaks

Run, boy, run.

The ears perceive certain extremely loud crashing noises which, again, cause the legs to move as if peddling a bicycle downhill with a strong tail wind.

Race, girl, race.

Again and again and again. *Boom, boom, boom. Peddle, boy, peddle.*

My partner plunges right down into the escape gully.

Into the loose clay and schist, with mammoth keep-on-truckin'-steps, the gully steepens and we use jump turns and ape-man muddy lunges, technique not graceful but speedy.

The descent slides and slops on. Snow gives way to drizzle. It's still a long distance to the upper basin, not to say the valley floor.

Because there has been no lightning for some time now, we relax a bit.

Crick, Crick, Shee. KABLAAAAAAAAM!

A big honking bolt wallops some up-there ridge. Fear returns. Down and faster again we scuttle.

Then, just the dismal falling rain. No more sudden gusts of wind, just a miserable trudge down the soggy slopes.

We pass a couple of big boulders and decide to take a breather and try to get out of the rain. We shake off our parkas. We don disposable ponchos and a tarp to drape over our legs. The boulder gives us some protection. We're sure the drizzle will let up now. It has to. We don't talk much in our wiped-out stupor. It's still a long way to the foot of the basin. We promise to move if one of us gets cold. For an hour we sit and wait, getting colder. Disgusted with it, we decide to simply carry on, through the rain.

RED STONE HEART

Back at camp, robins are busy in the meadows along the serpentine West Fork. We hang up our sodden rain gear, change out of our red mud-caked boots. Backed by lodgepole and open to the west, we can't see Tokewanna from our camp, which is fine. We can see Beulah, and the sun smiles down on us. Whether or not we see one or a pair, the wide-stretching willowy landscape before us is sure to boast moose, and they'll be out and about later. Squirrels chirp and clamber in inane territoriality, and we toss pinecones at them as we brew up coffee and rest on our laurels. Tokewanna, ka-ching. Tokewanna, never again. Tokewanna, *No mas, por favor.* Toke-a-wann-a never-again-a.

Tee goes off to fish, and I go off to gather firewood and feel sorry for myself.

Later Tee lays two trout, nice ones, a brookie and a cutthroat, on a log, and smiles his Hey-Dad-look-what-I-caught Grin. We get a fire going, cook up a mess of Lipton noodles, and bake the trout in aluminum foil with margarine and spices.

The next day's weather agenda calls for rain. Also rain and more rain. We guess we'd had a window, narrow as it was.

Tee gets tired of swerving to avoid the chocolate-milk-colored puddles everywhere along the muddy trail, so as the hike out drags on, he takes the *direttissima* and walks straight through the puddles, quite pleased with himself for reasons of efficiency. We had waded the West Fork bare-footed and gingerly at the beginning of our journey, but at the end we both stride boldly across slip-sloppy and fully shod.

Neither of us seems intent on going back to the valley below. We sit in his car and sing along with *Blood on the Tracks*. We watch the rain. "Idiot Wind." "Tangled up in Blue." "Lily, Rosemary and the Jack of Hearts." Tee and Tokewanna. I wish there was something I can do to get my mind off it. Climbing Tokewanna is good clean fun but it changes nothing.

It rains all the way to Richmond. My cat Lamont seems glad enough to see me. Just us two now. They'd taken everything I'd put out in the living room. She'd never even been there, really. All mine and Lamont's.

Tracks

It's easier to see critter tracks on snow, and that's why you see them.

Of all the tracks, bobcat are the most common, paws down. We ski or shoe in the same places. They're big enough to leave a good track.

While breaking trail, you will follow their tracks. And if you return after a storm, you will see that the bobcat used your old tracks, too.

Rabbits aren't that hard to find and trail if you're really hungry. Elk, moose, bambi, and porcupine are around leaving signs. Maybe you'll see the small paw pocket of an ermine, or the wider-digit tootsie-sign from a fox, weasel, marten, or the comparatively-big trench of the snowshoe hare.

Cougar tracks will be observed, especially on snow. Old tracks don't mean a cougar isn't around. You might find a cache up in an old burn, and look, there's a deer buried beneath the snow, and a little while later, another. It doesn't mean you ought to sit and wonder, wait for the cougar to return, decide if it wants to share with you. Your sign and scent will stir it up powerful strong.

Bobcats know the wind scours, spruce hollows and quiet places to spend time, out of the storms. It is right to share a track with them.

Larry-Like-the-Wind

Larry Darkness in his prime was like the wind. No one could keep up with him, and he wouldn't wait for anyone. This is a good characteristic of a solo climber, and Larry was often Larry-by-Himself, even when he was nominally with a group. To walk with Larry was to walk alone. Speed is safety, surely, but it can be argued that safety can also be found with a group, with enough people for someone to remain with an injured party, and someone to go for help. The true solo scrambler, such as Larry-by-Himself, doesn't account for going for help.

Stories of him in the Larry-like-the-Wind mode were many. A favorite takes place in the red rock country. On the way down from the Anthill, a bristlecone-topped, two-hued sandstone peak just south of Thousand Lake Mountain, in Wayne County, Utah, Larry-by-Himself got ahead of the four of us, myself, Marie Midwah, Gen. Disaster and Tee Trundler. He didn't wait for us. Nothing unusual on either count.

We followed his tracks that eventually led to the edge of a cliff. We looked all around the ledge, examined possibilities from all angles, and couldn't figure out how he had gotten down it, unless he had sprouted wings, as there seemed no reasonable way. To be safe, we traversed wide right on the ledge, then dropped down on talus and found our way eventually to the sandy flat. It was pretty remote country, this route from Sunglow to Sand Creek, up on a middle layer you really can't see from below.

We started heading northeast across the sandy flat, and soon we came upon his tracks. We looked back and were able to see that there was indeed a steep, narrow gully that would have led directly down the cliff from the ledge we had been on, a steep, straight and very-Larry gully, the way he must have gone. We cursed Larry-by-Himself, as we had lost half an hour in our safer detour.

As we continued walking, we soon noticed that right on top of Larry's tracks, easily visible in the soft sand, were mountain lion tracks. Quite large and extremely fresh puma sign, the tracks of a mountain lion that was stalking Larry-by-Himself as he walked across the sandy flat not twenty minutes ahead of us.

Looking at the minutes-old tracks of a fully-grown, mature, adult, veteran, super-sized cougar, we imagined that he or she might be sampling the stringy Larry just now: ripping him open easily, gizzard to yin-yang, gnawing upon his rich internal organs and coating cat whiskers with fresh warm blood. We pictured the cougar as it soundlessly charged him on the reddish sand, and pounced, and pounced again, and brought him down, tossed him around like a puppy with a sock in his mouth, and then went for the arterial or tore Larry's head clean off.

We began, at that moment of sudden recognition and clarity, to make much noise to discourage the lion from doubling back and investigating us. To let it know that we were around. To send it somewhere far, far away. Much noise as well as much tossing of rocks and tree limbs, as well as singing, and shouting about the ways of mountain lions. They shy away from such noise generally. You can count on it.

All the way across the half-mile flat we followed the tracks of the lion that stalked Larry, and we made much noise. We carried short stout limbs as cougar-handlers in case of feline trouble *mano a mano*.

We weren't sure if we'd find Larry-by-Himself as Larry-Strewn-about-in-Pieces. We knew we didn't want to meet this big cat as Cougar-Leaping-from-a-Tree. We scanned the trees of the pygmy forest. At the edge of the flat, we found bare-rock bulges, and we rolled a rock or two down the escarpment, hoping again to influence its behavior, just to be certain. Head for escape terrain, you hear! We got that clear between us now?

Hours later we finally caught up with Larry-by-Himself along Sand Creek. No, he hadn't noticed the lion, hadn't heard anything, really, or sensed that he was being watched and stalked, or about to be killed. He thought he might have heard some rock fall but had no idea that he had been tracked by one great big kitty.

Lanky as could be, exceptionally thrifty, Larry Darkness spent his student years at the Norwegian University of Utah living on something below the bare minimum. He walked everywhere and lived where he could walk everywhere. He lived in basement apartments and, on two occasions, he rented furnace rooms — at least they were warm and could be had for fifty dollars a month, plus a share of utilities. This is one of the ways he got his Darkness handle. He was willing to live in the darkness because Larry was not fond of working. He found that not working and living on nearly nothing made him happier than working. Working made him very unhappy. His major was physics with a mathematics minor. He got by on scholarships and a tincture of help from his stingy parents.

He always had the worst gear, too: third-hand and worn out and woefully inadequate and always in need of improvised repair. Gear that he called by naughty names.

I won't comment on his first backcountry ski outfit except to say that edgeless wonders and ski mountaineering bindings don't go well together. He liked to bomb a slope, lay down marvelous figure elevens, and upon reaching terminal velocity, Larry-in-the-Airy would leave the snowy earth and sail through the crisp, clean high-mountain air for remarkably long periods, before landing in violent, spectacular crashes when the mountaineering bindings would occasionally release.

When it came to ski-touring, Larry was

great to have around to break trail. The drill was simple. Everyone else would take a turn furrowing the fluff, but invariably Larry-Breathing-Smoke-and-Fire would grow impatient with the poky pace and demand to be out front. Fine. We let him blow by. Breaking trail is similar to bicycle racing in this way: the others can draft the leader, though a trail in powder gets easier with each passing person, so for the fourth person, it's a walk in the park. Impatient and out front, Larry-by-Himself could outdo anyone, and we let him.

Eventually by the late 1980s he had cobbled together some half-way decent gear, but his binding-skis interface was screwy, his gaiters never zipped properly, his poles were ratty, mismatched and bent, and his anorak would have shamed a transient. His rucksack sported a variety of holes and abraded spots, and his tent blew over one night at Arches.

Even with poor gear, his skiing technique could be an exquisite and powerful parallel, the result of having learned on the white asphalt of the Finger Lakes of New York State. Not wanting to drop the knee in the throw-back genuflect, he never really took to telemark. He kept his legs together.

Larry was also the least rounder of the regular crew: drank but lightly, and never went out to lunch. He was simply odder than hell, which is a little like the pot calling the kettle black, granted. *Hey, Blackie.*

He got summit fever earlier and worse than anyone I ever knew. He wasn't a weenie about it and never said, "What took you so long?" or "You have a problem back there?" or "I've been like waiting quite a while, Dude; it's good you finally showed up." He just took off, like the wind. He didn't pause or look back.

Now, this type of Larry-by-Himself behavior generally makes for poor wilderness etiquette. Yet you always knew what you were getting with Larry Darkness. He helped with camp chores, always carried more than his share of group gear, and wasn't much of a boaster. He was just faster than anyone. I think in some ways the mountains presented problems to solve for him, formulae to puzzle through.

True, at the time of the Lovenia adventure and in his third decade, Larry was a bit slower than in his salad days, but he was willing to try anything.

Jones
&
the Dumbest Traverse

I've seen the top of the mountain, Beavis...
and it is good.

Three weeks after Tokewanna I make an appointment with Larry Darkness to meet at the East Fork to try for Mount Lovenia. Looming at the head of the East Fork Valley, Lovenia is a peak with size and presence: an imposing pyramid, hard to reach, way back in there. The state's fifth highest officially named peak, Lovenia is surrounded by a panoply of towering business: Tokewanna, Tokeanother, and Wasatch on the west, as well as a dozen nameless high peaks and pinnacles to the east, all over twelve thousand feet.

From a distance Lovenia's shape is as pleasing as imposing. Its looks say *Mountain. Big mountain. Much prominent.*

Seeking to keep my compartments independently functioning, I arrange the Lovenia excursion to be a reward for some unpleasant matters in conjunction with meeting a Cache County judge in Logan, Utah, to finalize the divorce.

Although I have family roots in Logan, to be entirely honest, I'm not enjoying a warm feeling toward Logan in early July 1992, nor, to be frank, much of anything.

Following the legal arrangement, I go up to the Utah State University campus to meet briefly with my anti-therapist, Ben Adams, a fellow graduate student who is perhaps even more troubled than I. We talk about how life sucks generally and sometimes in particular.

I actually had a real therapist, who tried to get me to stop "compartmentalizing," but we had broken up a month previously. She was right about several things. The problem was that she didn't know exactly how to put it. She knew I was a mess, no fun, unnatural, overly self-focused, tedious and perhaps a bit ridiculous, but rather than saying "Behold, the river, Grasshopper. Become one with its flow," she got into the compartmentalizing analysis. She failed to realize that compartmentalizing is how someone like me survives. I keep things hidden.

But really I needed mentor, such as my good friend Xerxis Boga, who used to say, "Kevin, it does not matter." I needed to carry this succinctness around, keep it in mind, but instead I was carrying a rucksack full of baggage I had put there myself. I had gotten out of the habit of listening.

On the bright side, so glum do we appear, Ben and I, lolling about on the quad in summery sunshine, sporting our little rain clouds and ogling the student body, when a senior faculty member, Will Pitkin, strolls by, offers salutations, addresses our pale presences and is kind enough to dispense this little nugget.

"Don't worry, you two. Winter's only a few months away."

Ben gives the appropriate response, featuring a gesture, a dirty word and the personal pronoun "you!"

Enough of misery in the sun, I'm off for adventure, zipping up Logan Canyon in my sporty Toyota Celica, Jones. Jones is well past its prime. I had traded labor for Jones while working construction the previous summer in Park City. Working construction in Park City gave me grounds to try to get my life together, to motate my sorry ass to graduate school, to try to finally learn how to write good, listen better, and perhaps also get me a teaching credential.

Jones is one of those beater cars that require an owner to check the gas and fill the oil. Jones both burns and leaks oil in large amounts and needs some work. As a graduate student in American Studies and creative writing, I'm in no position to do anything more than drive it around fast when I can. Norah got the truck, and it was a pretty nice truck, and the dog. Of course, I got the cabin, the cat and this car, but that's another story.

From Logan Canyon, I roll past Bear Lake,

then through the green dismal pastures of Rich County, and into Wyoming's windy embrace at the scruffy border town of Evanston.

In these days I may have had a low opinion of the Cowboy State based on a variety of prejudices. Wyoming is the state one drives through to get to the Uintas or the Wind Rivers, not a good staying place. I don't have a good deal of experience with southwestern Wyoming, nor do I ever dream that I will someday reside here.

Somewhere on the Interstate hills between Evanston and Fort Bridger, I first perceive billows of gray smoke issuing from the rear end of Jones. This result is just a matter of the car being a little hot, surely. Just a teeny splash of oil on the manifold. Certainly. And it is a fairly warm day, after all. Smoke. Gray smoke. Clouds of gray smoke are not an indicator of anything, really. Smoke: gray smoke, clouds of gray smoke are nothing to worry about, sort of like a wife who spends an inordinate amount of time at one's best friend's tumbled-down hacienda.

Exiting the Interstate as planned at Ft. Bridger, I am also able to see a continuity of gray smoke, as it were, following me. Yet still, as if magically, I look the other way as I roll through Fort Bridger and Urie.

The rural landscape looks especially lovely in its early summer raiment and the snow-capped peaks beckon. From time to time I see the occasional pedestrian or townsperson pointing at me in passing, but I assume that everyone in this part of Wyoming stares, and Celicas aren't exactly as common as big and beautiful pickups.

The supermarket in Mountain View I remember as commodious and well-stocked from previous visits, with dead animals on the walls and friendly cashiers.

I purchase a couple of quarts of very fine motor oil. These I add to the crankcase. Jones burns oil and surely this is the cause of the smoke. *Just a tad thirsty, eh Jonesy?* Underway again, I notice that the two quarts haven't curbed the smoke, or maybe they have, it is hard to say just now. Yes, certainly, everything is under control. All compartments are successfully operating, all tray tables are in the upright, locked position.

As I roll onward, not too fast now, I hold tight to two ideas. First, air temperature drops the higher one climbs. This is well known, there's no question about it. Driving up the gently-inclined dirt roadway toward the East Fork, Jones will be blessed by the cool air which tumbles down from the mountains, and Jones' troubled motor will be soothed thereby. Second, things can't get worse, not today.

Robertson, Wyoming, is one of the most picturesque hamlets in the state. Rolling through this sweet-meats place, I begin to feel a warm rush of confidence. Jones is still going, running strong and reliable. Sure, there is still that pesky smoke, but the high hills are in view now, beyond the foothills, practically beckoning.

"Hello, Kevin. It is good to meet you. My name is Lovenia, Mount Lovenia. Why don't you come on up here and climb upon my rubescent slopes and shapely ridges and tread my cloud-catching top? Please feel free. I would like that very much."

The road winds through green meadows with stands of noble spruce and copses of freshly-leafed aspen. Moved by the surroundings, I decide to purchase a few hundred acres for my own personal use on the way back from Lovenia.

A couple miles past Robertson, a junction presents itself. The road straight ahead soon becomes gravel, passes over a creek, climbs a high bench, then descends into the ghost town of Piedmont, noted for its extant nineteenth century charcoal kilns that rise breast-like from a meadow. In any event, this would be the wrong road to take.

Instead, I take the hard left at the cattle guard. This follows the sign that reads, Wasatch-Cache National Forest, Meeks Cabin Res. 13. This is the way to the East Fork.

I scan the rear view then slow Jones down using a combination of brakes and down shift, rattle over the cattle guard, and feel the warm touch of elation. Now it is only a matter of twenty-five miles and I will be in the sweet-scented realm of spruce and fir, at the trailhead itself, the gateway to the East Fork.

I romp on the gas pedal and feel nothing. I re-romp. Nada. Nothing, as in nothing. The steering becomes leaden. The radio cuts out. The fan no longer fans. I put Jones into neutral and coast to a stop, pulling to the side of the road.

With the idea that Jones is not currently running, two thoughts swamp my mind. First, none of this is happening to me. No, it is happening to someone else, like or unlike me, it doesn't matter, but in a parallel universe, say, or in another time. Not ever. Not me. Not now. Nuh uh. Simply not happening. Second, Jones will start right up. Maybe after a brief rest. Start right up. Go Jones, go. Vroom and vroom.

RED STONE HEART

After five or perhaps eight minutes a reasonable person will be forced to retract the second thought above. No, now that you mention it, Jones is actually not going to start. Not now. Maybe not for a long time. Jones has some major mechanical problem[s].

Let's pretend that Jones has a dead battery. I simply get myself to an auto parts store, purchase a new battery, get back here, and then install it, using my handy tool kit consisting of pliers, a few wrenches, a couple of screw drivers, and a roll of duct tape. I know I can install a battery, and within an hour's time, we'll be underway again.

And yet I know that Jones' major symptom: a sudden, complete loss of power has nothing to do with Jones' battery. No, it is a deeper and a more serious problem, not a good or easy-to-fix problem.

In trauma it is good to try to maintain calm and control over one's self. This quality, indeed, can be critical to survival in extreme situations. When a person in trauma is calm and in control, triage may begin: an assessment of treatment and options is possible. What separates survivors of trauma is this ability to be both calm and to think clearly, to make a decision, even if it's the wrong one. It is imperative to act, to do something, not to be frozen with fear.

When I get out of my car, I calmly assess that my present location is in the country. A pleasant country, country at the foot of lofty mountains, not exactly in the center of civilization. Not, say, Washington Square Park at 2:00 p.m. on a Sunday in springtime. In fact, it is quite deserted. But I like and enjoy the country, often seeking it for peace of mind and social distancing.

Scrambling High Unita Peaks

What's more, I do have plenty of food, water and equipment to survive in the wilderness. In fact, I've brought a few extra quarts of acqua along, just in case. Survival, then, is not the issue. (In the year of 1992, no one had heard of a cell or satellite phone.)

I am not hurt nor in any great danger of getting hurt. The weather is fine, even balmy, with a light breeze and not too many buzzing, biting insects. There is little chance of earthquake, blizzard, rockfall, tsunami, lightning or avalanche on the road, here. I'm not all that tired. No members of my entourage are in any danger; my cat is safe in Richmond. I have no other members of my entourage, actually. I remember the morning: see the divorce court judge — that rear view is now my front view. "You're screwed, son" is gently flashing in neon up ahead. No objections made. Stamp and sign. Sign. Stamp, sign, goodbye and good riddance.

Um, you know, things are not really as bleak as they might seem. Sure, I've just gotten divorced. Just this morning. Yes, my wife left me for my former best friend. Oh, and by the way, yes, my car has just died. It has shuffled off its mortal coil and it has died. But my friend, Lawrence "Larry" Darkness will be waiting for me at the trailhead.

He will be driving in from another way, however, on the North Slope Road and he won't pass this cattle guard. True, Larry will be driving a very old, rusting-out Ford pickup, but Larry Darkness has mechanical skills, owing to his antediluvian rig and his inclination to fix rather than to buy. Therefore, so long as his old piece-of-garbage rig is still rolling, why, he'll be able to help me fix Jones somehow. Good little Jonesy. And Larry is not a flake. Just last night we'd talked by telephone and touched-up our plans.

It dawns on me that my best strategy will be to go find Larry. I notice, however, that I can't fit Jones in my backpack and carry it up to the trailhead. Nor can I push the turd-brown machine all that far. I do manage to get the car a few more inches off the road, but I notice that covering twenty-five miles will be out of the question. It is quite a rocky road, too, not really good for pushing in sections.

What will happen to Jones if I leave it? 1.) The car will be hot-wired and stolen—not real likely. 2.) The car will be pillaged, ransacked and then destroyed by some marauding Wyoming highwaymen or highwaywomen—do me a favor, buddy, please. 3.) The car will soon ascend into heaven, as none of this is happening to me. 4.) The car will be towed to an impound lot by the nearest civil authority. 5.) The car will be right here when I get back with Larry Darkness. Of course, it will.

I lug Old Brown, my backpack, out of the trunk and consolidate the rest of my junk into a tub, check my beautiful hair in the mirror, feel to make sure I have the keys in my pocket, and then face the turn and cattle guard, backward, sheepish and cheesy of grin, hoping to flag down someone, anyone, who has the bad luck to be driving by.

By Jove, it isn't five minutes before a young woman drives by in a small Plymouth hatchback. My main goal is not to appear crazy or dangerous. I stroll calmly over and say, "Hi. Thanks for stopping. My car seems to have died. I have a friend who's going to meet me at the East Fork. He's coming in over the North Slope Road. Um, you know, I kind of need to meet him. Is there any chance you could take me up the road as far as you're going? I'm sure I can get a ride from there."

She believes me and asks me in.

"Get in the car," is my self-talk. "It's okay to compartmentalize. Don't act crazy. You showered this morning. You haven't been drinking. Hell, you quit drinking, remember. This could be a pretty good test. You haven't been smoking. Just play it cool. Don't scare this poor girl."

"Thanks for stopping."

"Sure," she says.

"Well, listen, it's not exactly what I planned on," I say.

"Don't worry about it."

"I really appreciate it."

"Well, I've got to drive up there anyway. We live up there."

"Really? You live up there. Wow."

We have a pleasant conversation for a dozen miles. Her family has a cabin up the canyon and a house in Green River.

At the family cabin, she goes inside to talk to her brother. He comes out after a while wielding his fishing pole, opens up the door to his like-a-rock Chevy pickup, and tells me to toss my stuff in the back and get in. He tells me he'll take me all the way to the East Fork. His truck smells nice from the air freshener and cologne. We bounce up the very rocky road to the East Fork in near silence.

Near the trailhead, we run into Larry Darkness and his sorry rig. My driver looks at me with wonder. "Good luck, dude."

I dig a ten spot out of my thin wallet and hand it to him.

He pushes it back.

"No really," I said. "Go buy your sister a nice dinner. Please, I insist."

"You stop by sometime, you hear," he says. "We don't get too many visitors—tell us how your climb went."

"You're been very kind. Thank you."

Larry builds a modest fire to ward off the chill at 9,350 feet. A strong and unmistakable numbness settles over me. I can't think straight. I wish I hadn't quit drinking. If I think about it too much, though, it makes me want to puke. Larry builds the fire up to personal-privilege size. He sings in irreverent ways. He talks about his trusty truck. Suddenly I realize that I love his truck. My deliverance, as it were. I love it very, very much.

We trudge up the East Fork and make a base camp in its wild upper reaches, on a grainy rock shelf above the creek. Early the next morning, we walk up trail-less meadows to the head of the valley, the base of the northeast face.

Larry Darkness and I stop and consider our options up Lovenia. The east ridge terminates at a high col that connects to an unnamed peak. The north-east face, the only direct route, seems to be an imposing mess, alternating cliffs with taluses and layers of schist, and it doesn't look good. It seems like the kind of place to avoid unless thousands of feet of steep and loose rockslides and rotten cliffs hold great appeal.

It puts us into a bit of a quandary. A north-east face direct is out of the question. The only sensible option has to be to aim toward the high pass between the east ridge and the unnamed peak. We believe that if we head up a few suggestions of grassy slopes until we are quite high, then traverse under beetling cliffs, we'll be even with the col and able to work our way over to it. Surely the traverse will not be pleasant but how long can it possibly take? Fifteen or twenty minutes, max. To get up the suggestions of grassy slopes, an hour, tops? We're certain to be up on top before the lightning strikes of noon.

This would be a good time to discuss foreshortening.

Foreshortening is the appearance mountains have of not seeming to be as high as they actually are. All mountains are foreshortened, especially up close, at the base.

As you stand at the bottom of a peak, the close slopes seem longer than the higher slopes, which are foreshortened, when in fact the upper slopes are just as long as the lower slopes or longer, often longer, quite a bit longer. Because all mountains are foreshortened, novices and foolish scramblers underestimate the time it will take to reach the top.

If that example isn't clear, then take a tree, especially a big spruce or fir or pine, a redwood or sequoia. When you look at a big tree from a couple hundred feet away, the tree seems to be more or less as tall as it really is, its various parts displayed in proper, accurate proportion. Stand at the bottom of the tree, though, and the lower parts of the tree seem much longer than the upper parts. But they aren't. This is the trick of foreshortening.

Larry Darkness and I know this quite well. We've climbed numerous mountains together and apart. We've stood at the bases and wondered, and known that the upper slopes are long, very long, not nearly as short as they appear from the bottom and still made bad choices. We've been caused to suffer for this knowledge.

We don't let such knowledge get in our way today. Nope, we work up the lower slopes, up suggestions of grassy slopes, which are far more gravelly than grassy and far more rocky than gravelly, and far more suggestive than real. It takes us a long time to get up the lower slopes. It takes an even greater time to work through the middle slopes.

The slopes have steepened and the boulders have thickened. What lies between us and the col is nothing but large loose Mortality Makers on their various angles of repose. The lightest butterfly touch will move them. The traverse is going to be ghastly.

One of the great beauties of being in high mountains is finding a more appropriate sense of scale. Halfway up a ridge or out on some red rocky loose face, one's sense of self ought to be diminished. This effect is easily increased when one's companions are a long way off, appearing as specks on the snowfields or talus. Here we are nothing. Mountain climbing ought to engender a kind of humility. You may think you're pretty hot stuff, yet from the right distance and perspective, you ain't diddly. In fact, sometimes a little bit less than diddly. *I am less than much. Mountain is more.*

Scrambling High Unita Peaks

This more appropriate sense of personal scale ought to lead one toward humility, and then added to humility is its perfect grounds or proof: not merely are you not much, but also you have gotten yourself into a bad situation through simple foolishness or stupidity. Yeah verily, you have been a Dumbass, of the tribe and clan of the Dumbass, of the inclination of Dumbass.

Behold high on the slopes of Quandary Peak, Larry and Kevin Doubledumb waddle through thigh-deep passages of medium-to-large reddish-purple Blocky Shifters and sharp thigh-crushing Mortality Makers: quartzite boulders by the thousands. Watch the rocks move as the Brothers Doubledumb fight their way across.Fade out and note a vast sea of steep talus. Talus, talus, talus. Boulders, boulders, boulders. Steep, steep, steep. Dumbest, dumbest, dumbest.

Switch to a wide shot where the two are seen only as tiny dots, tiny dots moving in a sea of red and purple.

The air is thin at 12,300 feet, the terrain scintillating in its wiggle. No, Larry Darkness, it will not take no fifteen minutes. No, Still-Relatively-Young Kevin, more time will be required than one-third of one hour.

Now a close-up of a Blocky Shifter coming close to a scrambler's thigh. Brothers Doubledumb may get a good femur fracture for their trouble, a deep rumbling incessant pain, or a meaningful tib-fib snapdragon on a bad turn, with skin pierced, bones[s] bulging into the open air, a new wound dripping and oozing blood and strangely clear liquid onto the rocks, onto the grainy quartzite.

The Brothers Doubledumb may require helicopter evacuation.

It takes so long to complete the Dumbest Traverse that the world seen from East Lovenia Pass is now ominously threatening. What had begun as a warm humid morning has changed to a troubling noon. Most of Wasatch Peak is now hidden by droopy rainclouds. Kings and South Kings are both socked in. Distant thunder can be heard. Dark clouds scud. Here we go again.

What was clear and swelter now looks like storm and trouble. It looks bad, and the East Ridge of Lovenia is not a good place to be when the weather looks bad. It is a long and steeply exposed ridge. Seen that movie before. Acted in that movie before. Directed that movie before.

On the east ridge, a scrambler will be in Zeus-the-Thunderer's sights for much too long. A scrambler may be shown a fool traversing boulders but killed on exposed slopes.

Larry-like-the-Wind's solution is as elegant as fast. He goes ripping up the east ridge. He doesn't even wave goodbye. He just goes. Hell, it's close— very close—no more than an hour to the summit, maybe less.

I debate. I stew. I remember. I know that I have had many close scrapes, one with Mark Alpenglow less than five miles from where I now stand trembling. Had not Still-Fairly-Young-Kevin just learned this lesson yet again three weeks ago on the slippery slopes of Tokewanna? Learned yet again of the fear that comes from tumbling clouds and slashing electricity? The sprints of terror? The finger in the socket?

Even at Larry-like-the-Wind speed one is looking at an hour and-a-half in the open, as target, and chances are it'll be a crackly whiteout by then, and yet more time needed to get down to the valley below.

Rain would be a problem. Snow would be a problem. Lightning would be a big, big problem. One thing about the Uinta weather is that it always gets worse before it gets better. Always.

One closer bolt that busts up on the west ridge is all I need. *Bawk, bawk, bawk.* Wisdom is to learn from your mistakes. I round the corner, crab-walk down over the bulges, and start making my way down the north-east face. This proves a much better route, nowhere near as bad as it looks, a million times better than the Dumbest Traverse. There's a goat path in places. Surely other peak-baggers had come this way: down rubble-strewn clifflets bisected with crumbly chutes, all littered with rosy sharp detritus.

During the descent my bad side half-hopes that the weather will turn utterly dreadful. I hope to be running for [non-existent] cover from the plummeting dogs and cats, not to endanger my partner, Larry-by-Himself, of course, but bad enough to validate my decision, my decision to bail. Any minute now.... But by the time I make it to the bottom in a cloudy state, it is pretty clear that erring on the side of safety this time is the wrong call.

The weather is still sketchy, windy up there with some spitting rain and hail, but not that bad. Zeus-the-Thunderer hasn't rung our bell.

I sit at the bottom of the north-east face and

feel sorry for myself. To have come all this way just to turn around with the goal in reach—that isn't working. Sure, maybe it is prudent, but prudent don't get no gold medal. It also occurs to me there that nobody in the whole blessed world would have cared if I had gotten fried, or if Larry had gotten fried.

When he finally shows up, I do not ask.

No, whatever moose and elk we see, whatever trout I catch, whatever the beauties of the meadows we dawdle around in, whatever presentations are made of the rare beauties of the East Fork—and there are many—none of it can get me out of my pity pool. Larry Darkness finally seizes the carp.

As we're grubbing around with dinner, as if by the magic of the muse, Larry stands up, opens his cape and makes broad sweeping musical-theater gestures. Suddenly all the East Fork is a stage. Suddenly the trees are cheering, waving and cheering, and shaking their programs. A spotlight shines on us from the Dumbest Traverse. Larry then swishes anew and begins to interpret John Denver's "Country Roads." He begins on pitch, in tune, and double-time with a Dylanesque touch:

> *"Almost heaven, West Virginia,*
> *Blue ridge mountains, Shermandollup River,*
> *Life is old there, older than some trees,*
> *Younger in the morning, blowin' like a breeze..."*

Larry D. then slows down and heads for the chorus in perfectly bombastic overdone Broadway style, arms backhanding the air.

> *"Take me ho-o-o-o-ome, count-ry ro-o-o-o-ads,*

To the pla-a-a-ce, I beeeee-l-o – o-ng,
West Virgin-i-ia, Mountain M-M-Ma-maaa,
take me ho-oo-ome, lil' country r-o-o-o-oads…"
Before returning with,

"All my memories, gather 'round Herb,
Miner's Lady, stranger to blue water…"

I laugh till I cry.

Country roads? Where the hell do I belong? All my memories… Dack! Ugh! Where the Sam Hell is my Shermandollup River? How do I get there? I ain't got no herb and wish I had no memories.

Stranger to blue water? What's that supposed to mean? Huh? Is it a stranger to all water or just blue water? We are mostly water, so how can one be a stranger to…oneself?

Maybe not a stranger. Maybe not a blue-eyed stranger….

Since I have already bored you with the details of Jones's roadside afflictions, would you care to learn how the matter turns out? If not, please feel free to skip to the next chapter. If so, read on and make sure you have a tissue ready.

On the long hike out, my future life devolves into two possibilities. Jones will be where I left Jones or Jones will not. Both possibilities contain certain problems, and I'm not entirely sure which of the two alternatives is to be preferred.

Trudging through the East Fork's forests and many-moosed swards, it smites me that a deceased automobile is emblematic of and linked to an ended marriage, and symbolic, too, certainly, and that to leave both behind with some dramatic flourish might be useful, fitting and good.

The main problem with this thematic arrangement is that it leaves me without a mode of transportation, a significant problem since I live fourteen miles from where I work. On the other hand, a whopping repair bill doesn't sprout up in my mind like a swale of wild iris. I don't have too many stacks of hundreds beneath the mattress on the floor of my kickstand abode in Richmond, Utah. Finally, if Jones is magically still there, how do we get it to a garage?

Viewing the future's dim prospects keeps me from full enjoyment of the long walk out of the East Fork. Oh, and did I mention my sore knee and throbbing Achilles tendon?

Larry Darkness' pickup has rusted through in quite a few places, including through the floor on the passenger side. Old Whitey was manufactured sometime around the time of the Tet Offensive, and it honestly looks like two bags of groceries will redline it. We rattle down the rutted gravel road, grateful for each minute that passes and brings us closer to civilization.

In the end Jones is not there, waiting on the side of the road, manifestly not there. We must find him.

We head through Robertson to Mountain View. Upon learning that the sheriff's office is not in Mountain View, we proceed to the town of Lyman, Wyoming, a windswept burg with a fine view looking south and an overdone city hall. No one is in the city hall on a Sunday afternoon, of course, but a phone-booth call to the police dispatcher reveals that, yes, Jones has been impounded and is located at Such-and-Such's Garage.

There is no one at the garage, nor any contact address, so we look in the phone book to see if Mr. Such-and-Such has a listing, find that he does, drive around some more, and knock on the door of his *casita.*

The good Mrs. Such-and-Such informs us that, no, the little man is not at home, but he is around — he's out riding his bicycle. She tells us that, "He has a nice build but he's balding." This nugget is most helpful. We simply have to drive around Lyman, Wyoming, and look for someone who is riding a bicycle on a Sunday and has a nice build but is balding.

It doesn't take us long to find him. Lyman is not a very large town, but a fine town, all in all.

Mr. Such-and-Such has adopted the practice of dismantling the drive shafts on the cars he impounds to make sure he gets paid for the tow, which is certainly good business, we agree, as he explains this to us. He'll re-attach it just as soon as we get Jones up and running.

I'm not mechanically inclined. Larry Darkness, though, likes a good challenge and is soon looking at one. He has some tools, I have some tools, and also a tube of make-your-own gasket, so we survey Jones' cute little 2.2 liter motor, and decide we'll pull and then replace the head gasket, mainly because it's easy to get at, and so Larry gets busy and I stay busy feeling sorry for myself, feeling a bit shafted, so to say.

Once that job is finished, the head gasket replaced, we figure we're ready to give Jones a try.

We check the fluid levels. Surprisingly the oil is okay. We notice that the radiator is low. The good Mr. Such-and-Such lets us borrow some water and a water can, and we begin to fill up the radiator. Soon thereafter we perceive a robustly flowing stream of water issuing from a place it should not be pouring from. We notice, in fact, that this stream, this fountain of sorrow, is flowing from a fissure in the engine block. A large fissure. A crack. A crevasse.

When there is a crack in the engine block, the options become breathtakingly simple: junk the car or put in a new motor.

It is at this time that I begin to unload my personal possessions from Jones: maps, tools, papers, emergency supplies, and place them in the back of Larry's well-ventilated truck alongside our backpacks. Once that task is complete, I give Mr. Such-and-Such fifty U.S. dollars for his fine work towing the stricken Celica back to town. He signs the release receipt. Having no other choices, I then surrender the keys to Mr. Such-and-Such. I tell him I'll mail the title.

And then Larry and I drive away from Lyman, Wyoming.

By now, I'm sure that Larry is tired of hearing about it. I keep the catalogue to myself but do review it frequently. I have no wife, no car, no new peak gleaming on my Uinta list. Alpenglow is dead, Norah got the dog, and the truck (and it was a pretty nice truck) and all I have is a stuck-up cat, Lamont, some compartments, and a kickstand abode.

And it's all my fault.

Scrambling High Unita Peaks

Why worry? I do have a ride to Richmond. Things can only get better. They can't get no worse. At least I have something to write about...

And so it is that I don't return to the highest peaks in the Uintas for eight years, to let that trouble pass. That's not to say I stay away from the range entirely. Heavens no. I bag and re-bag some peaks on the fringes and ski the edges plenty but need to stay a good distance away from the red-rearing core, to be ready to find a way to approach it in different ways.

Ski Touring at S & M

Flat frozen lake, blue dome of sky, nude aspen trees, red rising cliffs, chickadees flitting among long-standing pines. We've been returning here for many years. It never gets old: Wrangler Peak, Dolly's, Yuri — an excellent icebox.

Larry and I reminisce about the day we skied all the way to Wall Peak and back. He recalls he broke trail most of the way, which is why my memory is fonder, why he remembers it so well. We talk about hollowing out the quinzhee (igloo), how warm it was inside the snowy womb: stove purring, candle dancing, how cold past midnight, slithering outside to tinkle, beneath a skein of stars, spruce and fir weaving the night breeze, and the storm that moved in by morning. Nothing tame about it. Yeah, that was great.

Scrambling High Unita Peaks

The quinzhee was fine shelter but a lot of wet work. Maybe there's a reason we didn't go back and do it that way again.

And then we remember the last time we visited: only a month ago, on a too-warm December day, and how the south wind roared, waved ridgeline trees, dark and free of snow. We could not ski but walked on bare dirt that smelled of distant spring. Streams flowed, un-iced, still talking: all this wrong for winter. At the bottom of Yuri Andropov Gully, we sat on dry boulders, rued our plight and started howling. Blondie the dog joined right in, a prayer for snow.

It must have worked. And how. Today three feet of fluff covers faceted snow, too much to safely ski the hillsides.

The delighted dog, white-snouted, disappears in deep drifts.

And like the dog, our tracks, deep snow, these blue-shadowed hours — all memories will evanesce, immaculate, unsung, except for leaving this.

Strange, But Not a Stranger

Some witnesses say that I seemed mopey during the disruptions of 1992. Mopey was only a part of it. I fostered the idea that if I ever got into another relationship, things would be different. I would be different and it would be different, because the only purpose of woe has to be to learn from it. The readiness was important.

So why does it call, "Go back to skiing?"

Living out in Richmond, Utah, north of Logan, there rose these nice sculpted foothills above town, which, when they filled in with snow, provided fine backcountry skiing. Naturally I skied by myself a lot, and sometimes with friends, sure, but mainly alone. It stuck me, standing at the top of a treeless bowl, looking into Idaho and ready to lay down some fine tracks that no one would ever see, that things couldn't ever get better than this: I'd never be a better skier with so few responsibilities, and at the same time, a little voice inside said, "Kevin, this just isn't enough." I fought with the left-right-left of it.

I'd wander around Richmond, lonely as a cloud, looking at houses but searching for a home, which could never be there, leaving little compartments behind me.

Who knew how long it might take? Would I be ready?

I'd seen Jennifer before, back at the Norwegian University of Utah, on the grounds by the Union Building, a lovely earth muffin, Ann and Nancy Wilson's little sister, with curly honey-toned hair and big green eyes. I stood stricken at the vision.

I think she smiled at me. I should have walked up to her and said, "I want to spend the rest of my life with you," but I was afraid. She would not have liked me then, in the throes of the Dead Baby years, given over to mockery and sarcasm. It ruined my day, this beautiful girl seen in passing, whom I figured was just a mirage, anyway.

How is it that ten years later she's taking the graduate fiction writing class at Utah State University? And how is it that she takes a vague interest in me, John J. Raincloud, when my life is falling apart?

We have a collegial lunch and she asks me all these questions about my marriage, which is crumbling, and my wife, whom I didn't understand, but for sure I don't want to talk about it. I find her nosy and a bit annoying. She even had the nerve to say that the story I shared with the class wasn't very good. It wasn't, being full of mainly exposition and plagued with a few axes to grind, but I thought it was great, so I didn't like that about her either. In those days, my wounded greatness was beyond reproach.

And then there was the time I observed Ken Brewer, the graduate director, give her a brief backrub in the writing lab. Being recently trained in harassment, I thought this was clearly a case of sexual misconduct, which I felt I might need to report. And this other faculty member, Bobbie Stearman, used to like to hang out with the other smokers and shoot the breeze. I would see Ken and Bobbie together at literary events and being a fish swimming alone in his own school, I thought of them as marlins.

But then Jennifer and I took the poetry class together, Ken's poetry class. Sharing work and interest, we got to know each other better. It turned out that Bobbie was her mother and Ken her stepfather. That kept things in the family and made them interesting. When she told me when her birthday was, I found it not to be funny. She had been born the same year and day as Norah, my ex. Go figure, a curse to a blessing, just like that.

To be frank, at this time her dress and style was far more professional than granola. Yet she'd grown up in Logan, skied at Beaver Mountain, explored the canyon and loved nature. In fact, with her ladylike ways and love of foo-foo things, she reminded me of my mother in good ways. Sister Dona had grown up in Cache Valley, too.

There could be a division of labor, surely, complimentary flavors. She liked nature, for sure, but a somewhat milder version of it. And we had many other things in common: words, literature, teaching. For myself, not ultra-keen on commitment at that moment, a single mother with children seemed way too complicated to take on. I always thought I wanted to have children, but children of my own, of course. It's not that I didn't want to be a step dad, it seemed like a pretty good compromise, but it just seemed tangled beyond complexity. Also, her ex was even more insane than mine, crazy insane.

So there was Needing-to-Get-his-Guano-Together Kevin, standing atop a ski run that no one else ever skied, facing north, looking toward not living in his own private Idaho while looking into Idaho, ready to do the left-right-left down a silky slope, wondering. It couldn't ever be enough, and in the end the tracks led one predominate way.

As Chekhov writes, "...It was clear to both of them that they had still a long, long road before them, and that the most complicated and difficult part of it was only just beginning."

And indeed, it took a few years and some twists and turns before we were able to tie the knot in Vegas in a ceremony that featured not only Elvis but a mini-concert and lecture by a rotund Elvis. The girls were horrified.

Fallen Leaves in the Night

Larry Darkness will take leave of us during the late nineties. The last trip we take together as Dead Babies is up to Indian Basin in the Wind Rivers. We hire mules to haul in (but not out) our gear, which is great, except that we bring in ropes and ironmongery for rock climbing, and I bring a small inflatable raft, pump, paddle and lifejacket to use to "bag" a very cold lake at 10,371 feet.

Before the fact, I predict that "lake bagging" may become a popular pastime. As with mountains, the lake has to be over ten thousand feet, and at least a few miles from the parking lot.

While it feels droll and invigorating to paddle the tippy craft around, and everyone takes a turn, it's clear that lake bagging has a couple of drawbacks. First, lakes that high are really, really cold. A dunk could lead quite quickly to hypothermia. Second, hauling the raft, paddle, pump and lifejacket out of the mountains, too, adds nearly ten pounds to the stone, and it's hard to see how lake bagging will catch on.

(Today new lighter gear tackles the second problem. The first, not so much.)

The hike out of the mountains we divide over two days. We set out with bulging backpacks, but Larry quickly disappears. We're fairly certain he's not ahead of us, since we didn't see him pass by or play through, and we would have. We wait for him several times, figure he's behind, holler and cuss, but he has vanished. This isn't exactly unusual, for Larry often disappears, but always ahead, not behind, and at some point he would wait, but this day he simply goes away. During the many waits, Tee, Durancos and I say unflattering things about him. We finally reach Hobbs Lake and spend several anxious hours waiting.

It just doesn't make sense. The trail to Island Lake and on to Titcomb Basin is one of the most heavily-used in the whole range. It has plenty of ups and downs, punishing ups and downs, but it's not a hard trail to follow, nor a trail one would be alone on for long. We figure maybe Larry, being Larry, set off cross-country as Larry-by-Himself or Larry-like-the-Wind. This is not a good scenario. None of us is as young as we used to be. It's not that difficult to get disoriented.

Larry-by-Himself shows up just as darkness falls. I find him first and inform him that everyone is pretty pissed at him and ask exactly what happened. He acts like it's no big deal and says that he'd just taken a wrong turn.

At camp Don and Tee join in with gnashing of teeth. Losing a member of the group can ruin a day, and it had, and grrrh. Larry plays it nonchalant. He eventually pulls out a map and tries to explain where he had gone. It is a ridiculous detour, way out of the way.

"Larry, didn't you notice that you were climbing there above Island Lake for, what, about two hours?"

"Two-and-a-half hours?"

"And that the direction you were headed —toward Cook Lake—was totally the wrong fooking way?"

"The wrong way. Wrong way Larry!"

"Larry?"

"Wrong way."

"Yeah," Larry says, "I started to figure I was lost when I got to the top of the pass... Not what I expected. Not at all where I thought I was. So, I guess I had to make pretty good time to get back here."

Tee and I remember the time Larry-the-Fearless-Leader took the totally inexperienced younger brother of General Disaster on a gruesome all-day-and-most-of-the-night death march, with a side of stream and glacier crossing(s). It cured the poor kid of ever wanting to spend any time in the high mountains.

Again, it is one thing to take a wrong turn, but another to follow your bliss and keep following it, when it is obviously not the right way to go.

The talk grows a bit more heated. Tee says that it's understood that when you're with a group, you're responsible for everyone in that group. What you do can affect everyone. And it's pretty much a given that in an emergency, everybody gets to help. Don and I second it.

"And we wasted a lot of hours today waiting, Larry," says Tee. "Waiting for you when you were out picking daisies or whatever."

"I didn't ask you to wait."

"You didn't have to ask," Tee says. "We waited because that's what we do."

"You don't have to."

"The hell we don't," say Tee and Don.

"Look, you guys," Larry says. "I really don't care for or ask for this…assistance. I'm not looking for your 'help.' I'm out here for adventure. I can take care of myself. I got back here in time, didn't I?"

"What if you didn't get back?"

"I did," he says.

"But what if you didn't?" we say.

"I guess I'd be on my own then, wouldn't I? On my own and able to take care of myself."

After a pause, Tee says, "Um, fuck you, Larry."

"Really, Larry?" adds Don.

"Fuck-a you," he says.

"No, fuck-a you!" It echoes.

No resolution seems possible, and it's a dispute that festers.

(It would have festered more fully if it hadn't been for the Incident with the Balloons which distracted us from our dispute. Sometimes party-time-is-here-again trumps conflict, and the Incident with the Balloons represents another story with a different thematic arrangement, which might deflate any idea of personal nobility and exemplary behavior, which is the goal of the present work, thus I can't go into it at this time.)

RED STONE HEART

Years later, Don Durancos, Tee Trundler, Sean McHelen and I find ourselves walking around Island Lake and find the wrong-way turn Larry had taken. While it is possible — remotely possible — to see why he had, it is also immediately clear that there is no major well-traveled trail that way. It's like trading a highway for an elk path. The "path" also begins climbing immediately after it leaves the lake, and it doesn't stop climbing for several trail-less miles. Nobody in his right mind would have seen it as a sensible way to go or a shortcut.

At the same time, we know that is the key. By the time Larry-by-Himself has gone on a detour, he's already on the walkabout. Larry-by-Himself is undergoing adjustment. Although always just a bit outside the box, it seems Larry has gone a bit too far into the dark and velvety side.

It seems, perhaps, that Larry's hold on this particular type of reality is evolving, and Larry one day just slips away.

Larry-like-the-Wind goes back to Ithaca, New York. All this time out West, it's difficult to say what it was to leave it behind. He goes back East and he has stayed there, mostly in Connecticut.

That, too, doesn't make much sense. Nobody loved the wilderness more than he did, and certainly not much in the East could match the West's mountains and canyons for size, scope and beauty, no offense intended. Maybe it isn't about that. Ithaca's pull is strong. Maybe he's still at it, undercover.

Sometime later, into the new century, Larry Darkness reappears in virtual form as Horatio Algeranon. Horatio blogs in the form of a mouse, writing Anonymusing Tales. More specifically, Horatio Algeranon, the blogging mouse writes rhyming couplets about (usually) global warming. Horatio is very well versed in all aspects of the topic, its features, fallacies, proofs and critics. And he sticks with it for years, long enough to be footnoted and discussed in the relevant literature. Cited, even and annotated anonymusingly.

As ever, he's a pathfinder. He knew how important climate change was and would grow to be.

Both as legendary slogger, as well as a blogging mouse and composer of heroic couplets of climactic nature, Larry Darkness/Horatio Algeranon remains without peer in this or any world.

Yes, I do hear from him occasionally, recently regarding basketball player Bol Bol and departed diplomat Boutros Boutros-Galli, not to mention Afghan politician Abdullah Abdullah, who was robbed.

Part IV
The Talus Palace

2000-2005

Talus: Noun. A deposit formed by an accumulation of broken rock debris, at the base of a cliff, on a slope or face, or in a chute or gully. Singular: We saw a pika in the talus by the tarn. Plural: Today we crossed a lot of talus. From Latin, ankle part or ankle. Syn. boulder field. See also German, *Felsenmeer*, sea of stones. French, *astragale*. Italian, *talo*...

Scrambling High Unita Peaks

Dogs on Peaks

*Only unleashed dogs can do that. They
are a kind of poetry themselves when they are
devoted not only to us but to the wet night, to
the moon and the rabbit-smell in the grass and
their own bodies leaping forward.*
— Mary Oliver, 2016

Dogs can be great companions. They will go
with you almost anywhere, won't talk back and only
occasionally balk.

Some dogs are better than others.

Scrambling High Unita Peaks

Lander is a large malamute with fine markings, a mellow temperament and a mind of his own. Lander is a fairly good dog mainly because Lander is not a really bad dog. On balance his goods outweigh his bads.

Still, Lander does like to go a-wandering. He isn't really a game chaser: a follower of moose, deer and elk, not to mention porcupines, as many really very bad dogs are. Rather he is given to aimless wanderlust. He doesn't like to be told what to do. Lander will come back. Often. Usually. Eventually. But in most things Lander is not a dog that's into following directions.

Most of Lander's freewheeling tendencies are a reflection of his hands-off owner, the elusive Don J. Durancos. It's not that Durancos simply gives Lander free rein to do whatsoever he pleases, it's more that he doesn't pay excess attention to his dog. They're cool with each other. They're cool with whatever.

Like his master, Lander is a seeker. Both are seekers after truth, adventure and experience. There's nothing Lander won't try, except obedience. As a dog he's often Lander-on-His-Own. It doesn't take long to ruin a bad dog. My mother-in-law can do it in forty-five minutes. To ruin a good dog takes more effort.

Let me illustrate this with a cherished memory of Lander. Picture a high mountain lake somewhere in the Rockies. Behold the olive-blue depths of a sunshine-brimmed body of water, ringed with well-sculpted granite shelves and clefts. The inlet cove is afloat with lily pads, a white sand beach strands between outcrops, and fragrant groves of spruce and fir sweep up to high ridges. And yes, that really is a seagull.

RED STONE HEART

This spidery lake's several arms stretch out. Watch a hatch of insects swarm across the calm water, seemingly smoke, enticing trout to roil the surface in a feeding frenzy. A marsh hawk wheels southward.

Such a scene provides a worthy place to halt, enjoy some talk and kibble. We humans need to rest — Don, Tee and me.

Lander-On-His-Own has wandered and now stands across a narrow bay from his owner. (Remember that Lander is a large and fine-looking malamute.)

As the rest stop draws to a close, Don J. Durancos begins calling unto his wayward dog.

"Here, Lander. Here, boy."

Don calls again. "Come on. La-a-ander."

Lander often assumes deafness in such circumstances. But not this time. Lander listens. Rather than trotting around the long arm of the lake to rejoin Don, Lander blithely plops into the lake and swims boldly toward his master.

It is good for Lander to be swimming across a picturesque lake in the mountains. "Good dog, Lander."

One thing, though: Lander is currently wearing a dog pack. Making Rover a temporary beast of burden makes up for much care and trouble. A medium-large dog can easily carry eight or twelve pounds and should, and the extra falderal functions as a secret weapon for the owner. Every ounce Spot carries makes my pack lighter and my steps happier.

As Tee and I watch this, with our dogs leashed and tethered (based on moist experience) we salute the noble Lander plying the sparkling waters, doing a fine dog crawl, head above the water, pack within, snorting stalwart obedience with every stroke. What a happy picture, with a swimming dog slurp-snorting its way toward its master. It just warms the cockles of your heart.

"You must be very pleased, Don."

Don nods grimacingly, like Clint Eastwood.

"Hell, I'm proud of Lander and he's not even my dog."

It must be noted that Lander's pack contains the following items: part of Lander's food supply, a pair of spare socks, a spare t-shirt, two packages of Lipton dinners, and granola bars for trail food. A several minute swim in forty-three-degree water soaks these items utterly.

When Lander finally makes shore, we ensure Don J. Durancos is not able to discipline his dog. He had called, "Here, Lander. Come here, boy."

Lander had simply obeyed. Good dog, Lander.

As Tee and I watch Lander shake the water off and Durancos unpack his sodden goods, we have to stifle some snickers. Some things do not belong in a dog pack, for instance, things that are meant to be dry.

Durancos, Tee Trundler and I have a pretty good thing going with our dogs in these days. There's Lander, a gelding, and two fine fixed-females, Blondie and Daisy. We have trained them to like to climb peaks. We have conditioned them. We have coaxed them over the bouldery sections and heaved them up short cliffs. We have addressed their counter arguments. We have brought them along and shown them the way.

In fact, during the 1990s and into the new millennium this canine trio finds itself on the summits of many, many peaks in the Wind River Mountains: over forty individual ascents between the three of them, Daisy, Blondie, and Lander. Yes, forty...over forty, actually. It seems bad form to boast about it, though, even on their behalf. Oh well...did I say over forty?

Next we will consider my dog, Blondie.

Blondie is in a few ways a fine dog. Handsome, well-proportioned, she is descended from Chesapeake Bay Retrievers with a tincture of golden retriever tossed in, hence her lighter color. Blondie is strong, brave and loyal. She has problems.

Blondie will go after any other dog, Great Pyrenees to poodle, and Blondie does not discriminate. She goes in teeth-bared for the kill. This causes some trouble in society: "May I have my arm back, Blondie?" "Sorry about what's left of your rat terrier."

Some of this inclination may well have been organic, but some of it came from her beginnings. In many ways, hers was an idyllic puphood and early youth spent on ranches in Caineville and Teasdale, Utah. Blondie's owners put her to good use by giving her the job of keeping all unwanted intruders out of the yard and off the property. Blondie learned not to be picky: cows, deer, horses, goats, ravens, hares, sheep, mail carriers, the Schwann's delivery man, flies, llamas, bison, songbirds—she chased them all away. Her vocation is to be territorial, and not a little territorial.

Scrambling High Unita Peaks

The Chesapeake is a working breed. Chesapeakes bond, if they bond at all, to one owner. They demand daily work and exercise. They are highly emotional.

Blondie also suffers depression and anxiety.

She has learned to be a family dog, sort of. But I would never leave her alone with a young child. Her favorite place may be to sit by the firepit in Good Water while teenage Jacque passes her a steady stream of roasted and unroasted marshmallows.

Blondie seeks diversion from her mental problems by binge eating—she is just dynamite on cookies—and by generally being disagreeable, sullen, moody, but very good looking. It's appropriate to also mention her strong case of claustrophobia: she pants like a locomotive anytime she's in a vehicle. Endless panting punctuated with light farting. Rides with Blondie are always a joy.

Lander's free-wheeling and devil-may-care attitude actually works well with Blondie's kill-anything-that-moves ways. They form the most annoying and energetic pair in canine history.

Tee's dog Daisy, a border collie, in comparison to the two reprobates, is a paragon of doggy virtue. She is actually a good dog, not a perfect dog, but a very good dog. Smart, possessing solid leadership skills and an innate ability to separate herself from the dopey dalliance of Lander and Blondie, Daisy knows herself to be the leader, and we are all the sheep. She likes nothing more than to gain the brow of a hill when we are kicking back, park herself some distance off, observe us and study the land, and all the little things living in it. Oh, and she can catch fish, too. Lots of 'em.

Tee's real-life job as a mechanical engineer enables him to acquire a stately Victorian on SLC's Fifth Avenue. Lady Trundler has the run of the house, generally, but added-on to the rear of the original house is a generous-sized room with bathroom. Often it functions as a guest room, but it is at its best use when it becomes Tee's map room. Later it will become Teemore's guitaritorium.

Both sides of the big Wind River maps are displayed on the walls, and fine little push pins are used to demarcate a peak which has been bagged. Over the years, the push pins grow in number and extent. There are also two Uinta maps with accompanying pins. Often we get in the right mood, look at maps, talk large and ludicrous, and do some puffed-up planning. It's a ritual that keeps us wanting to do something again together. All good trails lead out from Tee's map room.

Dogs on peaks, good.

Dogs on snow, good too.

It's great to watch them bound across the meadows, where the streams run still and braided, how they leap across the hummocks, silly dogs. Or chase each and every chipmunk and squirrel, never catching one. And act excited when get ready to go somewhere, pacing and nuzzling, but feign sudden incapacity, all stoved-up and whimpering, when we try to put the packs on them. Or to be grateful when, finally played out, our best friends lay down and rasp a few in camp.

The Posse

Solo hiking, scrambling and climbing is great. It's useful and inevitable to gain some experience alone. People who don't mind being alone are often called introverts. Rambling solo is inherently introverting because there is no one to talk to, but you still need self-talk to find a way through it, and you better pay attention to your surroundings.

When solo hiking, scrambling or climbing, one's experience tends to be more emotionally stimulating. Bear country is great for this, too, because it demands that the senses be over-alert: is that a squirrel caching nuts or a hyperphagic grizzly ready to charge? In skiing it ups the ante. Get buried and they won't find your body until, well...you know. Also, when you're alone, you can't blame anyone for your mistakes, but you will still try. And you don't have to wait. But if you mess up, you alone will pay.

Grizzly Man says, "Go ahead and suit yourself, but happiness is only real when shared."

RED STONE HEART

It's safer to go in a group and funner too. At some point, if you're lucky, you will have a regular gang of friends, people who are like-minded souls, co-adventurers. You meet along the trail. You might journey with clubs, outdoor programs, singles groups, churches. Maybe you ski around. A goal of mingling is someone to do it with and someone you can talk about it with afterward. In the debrief you share the memories, build on what you've learned and look forward with far-fetched plans.

When you go solo you break your own trail. But when you can share the duties, risk and fun, you are lucky indeed.

Just a few days after Jennifer's ex shows up at our door with a rifle and the intention of killing us, an attempt we thwarted but not without scars, with Katie and Jacque in tow, Jennifer and I move to Green River, Wyoming in 1997. Jennifer had landed a job at the local college, and I was promised employment as well. Though austere, the town is located between the Uinta and the Wind River ranges, making it even easier to venture to favorite places. It seems safe. We hunker down for some years in the Wild West of Wyo.

Don Durancos finds a home in Fruita, Utah. Trundler remains in Salt Lake.

Our son Christopher is born at the end of the next year.

Though we live in different places, Tee Trundler and I often join forces to take care of some protuberant business or other. I like to think I'm his favorite pardner. For sure he is mine. Every year we collaborate, often several times. We make a good team, perhaps more careful and experienced with a bit of seasoning, sometimes not—all right usually not.

We get along and complement each other's weaknesses. In some ways, of course, we magnify each other's weaknesses—what else is a climbing partner for? We like wild life, and we like seeing wildlife. We like getting lost but not too lost. We like to find a way down without knowing if it will really go. Back on earth we play blues guitar together. We take a stab at Otis Rush, John Lee Hooker. We do "Watchtower" to a mambo beat. He plays lead and I accompany.

Tee is a much better rock climber. Until he's close to forty, he completes many notable climbs throughout the West. He builds a climbing wall in the woodshed and, eventually, in the yard. Yes, in the yard. Fortunately, as he gets older, he moves away from the cliffs and shelves his nuts and rack. Peak bagging and backcountry skiing become his focus. He can always be counted on to act as guide on the ground, and he has an uncanny ability to find a way through nasty terrain.

My particular job is often to hatch ideas for peaks and trips and routes and drum up support for them. This evolves into the system we use.

For much of this period, often together with Durancos, we dedicate ourselves to the Wind Rivers, trying first to make it up some shapely and prominent peaks: Jackson, Fremont, Pronghorn, Gannett, Bonneville, Wind River, Temple, and once these are done, to try to pile up large numbers of other ascents. Tee comes up with the silly idea to have the number of Wind River peaks we've ascended match our ages, a target moving in the wrong direction every year, because ridiculous as it is, it gives a reason to get together and try to knock off a few more.

This becomes even more plausible when I move to Wyoming. Tee and I eventually reach this milestone and stay ahead of it for a while. But to mention it now seems boorish and self-serving. What's fifty-plus Wind River peaks? Raise your hand if you care.

By the end of the decade, though, we decide to refocus attention on the Uintas, and we begin to work toward the Notorious Nine. Then, realizing we can have both Wind Rivers and Uintas, we try to balance things in both ranges, and both work perfectly together, like vinegar and oil, coffee and Bon Jour, Led and Zeppelin, pizza and pepperoni, blue cheese and buffalo wings.

Still, it's not just about me anymore. Time away in a time of mounting responsibilities means a bit more planning, more negotiation, more pints of A positive donated when Daddy gets to go away to play.

To our gang of grizzled mountaineers, the young rookie Sean McHelen is added. A native of the Keystone state, at first McHelen knows nothing about slogging peaks. He gloms onto our posse and soon begins to learn things about pain, suffering and fear that he could not have imagined in his previous lives. We seek to mentor him.

When you start at zero, there's only one way to go. Soon Sean McHelen finds that he accepts our pointless hobby. He learns how to get lost, how to bring too much gear along, how to guess wrongly about the weather, how to walk for hours and get really tired. We show him an approach to adventure that is novel and intriguing, and a passion for the mountains of the Intermountain West.

McHelen has an odd matrix of abilities and skills one often ascribes to the idiot savant, with the emphasis being either on idiot or savant depending on the circumstances. With test scores in high regions, nevertheless common sense is often well out of his reach. This is why he would have been attracted to bagging peaks: There is obviously no good reason to do it. Its lack of sense compelled him onward and upward on many a catch-up day until he was able to leave his hoary elders in the dust.

In real life, though, he lands a job with Great Satan Industries, a firm that brings nuclear waste made elsewhere to Utah to bury. This brings a bit of fission to our worlds. We don't talk about it, though, since we have a hard time talking about anything that matters.

Tee, Kevin and Sean

Black Forty

2000. Wyoming campgrounds are preferable to Utah ones, with fewer people to impinge on the freedoms the Cowboy State enjoys. News went out for a mixing at the Meeks Reservoir. A bunch of folks have been invited for my Black Forty party, with the added goal of an attempt to ascend lofty Gilbert Peak, the third highest in Utah, just over the border from Wyoming in the Beehive State.

Gilbert Peak, a massive offset pyramid, is an unmistakable presence. It was named for Karl Grove Gilbert, an emcee and major dude in late nineteenth century geology. Gilbert peak is a worthy goal to revive our Uinta interest and celebrate four decades under the sun, as I hope to stand, No-Longer-Young-Kevin, Here-Comes-Middle-Age-Kevin, Kevin-with-a-Rolodex-Kevin, Family-Man-Kevin. What could be better?

Well, uh, my efforts to exert control over

too many individuals and events results in a bit of fraying around the edges. It is imagined that the ascent itself will involve experienced veteran Tee Trundler, the elusive Don Durancos, young rookie Sean McHelen, Suddenly-Middle-Aged-Kevin and some dogs. Others will enjoy more leisurely walks in the hills and meadows, sightseeing, feelings sharing and perhaps a bit of angling. D. Harry Menzies, fka Suleiman the Magnificent, will be in charge of the lowland business, as he has already ascended Gilbert. We will do our own separate things. What can be wrong with this fine plan?

Well, Tori Shoulders, an old friend, who was duly invited, shows up with her two charming teenage sons. This is great, kids are great, and kids should certainly be introduced to the wonders of the wilderness, it's just that Tori and her two sons decide that they want to tag along with us, to attempt Gilbert, and I've got few worries about this scheme.

Zeke Shoulders is all of twelve, and I'm fairly sure the proposed outing is way too long of a marathon of misery for this bright, skinny kid. Sometimes a first experience with the jagged edge of high country can form lasting impressions — best not to have the wrong impressions, surely. There isn't much worse than the pain inflicted when the body is nowhere near fully grown.

Nathan Shoulders is a strappling young fellow of fifteen, and certainly has the frame and size and stink and hair to do it, but it looks as though there might be some attitude issues with him, like he'll pull an attitude at altitude. Is he really going to enjoy hoofing it a dozen miles up to 13,444 feet, and then back down? It's hard to say, but the concept of this walk is not his, and that issue of ownership is sure to become clear. And not much is worse than dealing with mutiny or coaxing an unwilling young person to get-along-now-little-doggie for miles.

The entire Henry's Fork is a great corner of the world, certainly, and in late May, joy and rapture will be readily available.

There are plenty of good reasons not to commit, and solid grounds for turning back, but when two or three of us have made careful plans through months of incessant online babbling, and are tuned up and rocking, there just isn't going to be a lot of extra concern to go around.

Well-focused is inflexible. "You need poles? What do you need poles for?" Well-focused wants to get things done.

A several days backpack is arguably the better and easier way to take care of this peak. That's not our proposition. Looming Gilbert is not anything that can be done in one day unless it is an exceptionally long, well-focused and disciplined day.

I try to explain this to Tori Shoulders and the boys in a neutral, non-threatening way, such as, "I suspect we'll be out for at least twelve...or... fourteen hours, and walking all the way. Hey, you walk and then you walk all day! Hey, hey, my, my; walk all day and want to die."

No use.

If we can't convince Tori and her boys to bail, at least by demanding an early start, the problem may be solved.

Scrambling High Unita Peaks

Yet long before Dawn's rosy fingers drape the east in gold, we are all up and stirring. In the darkness preparations are made. Close to our planned departure time, we begin the lengthy drive to the trailhead.

As we drive in Jennifer's Cherokee, I try to continue expressing my qualms to Tee and Sean. Durancos is happily ensconced in the other rig. Don feels a shine toward Tori Shoulders, and she him, for he looks rather like a movie star, a thinner Clint Eastwood as Josey Wales without the coarse manners. And she does, too. Think a more petite Selma Hayek, and then some. They like spending time together. You know, they might make a very attractive couple, let's hope they don't attract paparazzi.

Tee and Sean are not interested in listening to my complications but rather with their focus.

"You got your headlamp, right?"

"You?"

"Headlight, matches, clothes and food, blah blah blah."

"Ice axe, ski poles, pants for the disco glissade, blah blah blah"

We're also planning on crossing the snow-swollen Henry's Fork River as a shortcut and have brought special designated footwear to use in the crossing.

The ride stretches. It's now fairly light out. Maybe I should give up trying. Nothing about this is good.

Just a couple of hundred feet short of the parking lot, Tori's compact sports-utility vehicle pops a flat tire. This puts us a vat of brine. If we diddle around to fix the tire, we might as well kiss our chances of getting back in daylight goodbye, maybe all our chances.

"Sorry…I know this is a problem, but…."

Tee, Sean and I kick the dogs out and scuff our feet at the surroundings impatiently. Time slows.

"Sorry to be jerks about it, uh, but we really have got to get going…"

The nearby spruce and fir stand fragrant and puissant. Chickadees and juncos twit in the cool morning air. Sagebrush wafts and phlox blooms in pink and white.

Don Durancos takes the helm and assumes control of the situation. He'll stay and do the repair work as needed, make sure it gets done right, makes sure we're long gone.

"You guys make the best of it, really," he says. "We'll get this stupid flat fixed up and go hike a little later, probably see you somewhere up there. Take whatever time it takes. Up the Henry's Fork Trail, right?"

Not wanting to risk any change of mind, we summon Daisy and Blondie back into the Cherokee and rip up the remainder of the road.

I offer ardent supplication: "Thank you, Lord. Thank you for hearing my prayers. Thank you for making Tori's car have a flat tire. Thank you for overlooking my many sins and transgressions. Thank you for ignoring my petty egotism and personality flaws. Thank you for giving Don this lucky break. Thank you for Zeke and Nathan Shoulders. Thank you for Tee and all his ways, and Sean, too. Thank you for the wonders of Bridgestone. Thank you that Jennifer is still in Green River and that this car's title is in her name. Thank you that I have brought some lightweight designated footwear for the stream crossing. Thank you that the morning suddenly looks a million times better. Thank you for the Uintas and their mighty cirques and ridges. Thank you for all of this and more."

Day packs shouldered, Tee, Stan, Daisy, Blondie and I are just about to set out when Lander shows up. We holler for Don, "Hey, Don, your freaking dog is up here,"

And Durancos hollers, "Lander, here boy. Come on now."

We wish to waste no time in our escape. Lander slinks off after a few more aspen limbs and rocks are tossed his way. Why wouldn't he want to join us? Daisy and Blondie are his crew. The large and lanky malamute has no interest in fixing flats or making conversation with the two boys. We storm up the trail. He disappears.

Maybe ten minutes up the trail, though, Lander-On-His-Own shows up, looking sheepish but looking ready for the duration. He isn't our dog. He isn't our responsibility, exactly. We're his owner's friends. He seems to understand this. He's with us now. He shadows us, not exactly close but not far.

We scarcely take a breather, hoping to put all the complications behind.

After a couple of hours on the trail, we deviate to begin the short cut. First, we must cross the icy stream, swollen by dirty snowmelt, squeezed in between grassy banks, using the designated footwear, and wielding ski poles for balance. We watch each other cross. We get the dogs across without complication, working as a team, anticipating their downward swim with strategic helping pulls out of the ice-nudged water.

We set off cross-country. The hard walking begins. The first hour features steep forest. The second hour boasts grassy slopes, limber pines and ridges. The next hours stretch on talus, a purgatory of low-angle Death Platters in every imaginable size and shape, and a damnable false summit, then another false summit, and yet another.

Finally, worn out from eternal talus and the exceedingly false summits, Tee, Sean and I gain the top, ready to rest. The weather's good until it threatens, and delivers, but just a short, warm spring blizzard without trouble or lightning. We sit it out on the summit, then make the best decision of the day to wrangle down the marvelous whaleback ridge that eventually spits us out at Dollar Lake. The ridge curves deliciously and drops steadily, providing grand views of the big red scalloped country. We enjoy another snow squall or two, a disco glissade, and all the early season spice: the purple-red ledges of Gunsight, the twin tips of Kings and South Kings, the deep trough of Henry's Fork: lake-strewn, greening-up and majestic.

Passing Dollar Lake we endure a fourth act of willows and wet bogs before finally rejoining the main trail to begin the six or seven mile death march back to the car, but it's a downhill march, and we'll make it by crawling if we have to.

Lovely in the lovely afternoon, we run into Tori, Nathan and Zeke Shoulders and Don Durancos in a meadow. Durancos is glad to see his dog. He wasn't exactly sure where Lander was but hoped he had gone with us. I'm happy to see them and learn that their day has turned out exactly as it should have: full of alpine splendor, good conversation, rich memories for her boys, bonding with an eye to the future, and much stimulating exercise.

And so, despite many false summits and wrong turns, the outcome of this Black Forty is clearly a win-win all around. Durancos grows closer to Tori, she him. Lander spends the day with his accustomed crew but without his master. Tee and I add another one to the stringer, an important one. Young-rookie Sean McHelen learns how much one can endure in twelve/thirteen hours. We learn new meanings of "a long day hike." Suddenly it seems that bagging all the Notorious Nine will be possible, in good style. Everyone gets back safely.

That night I get to hold my toddler, Chris, by the fire, which is pretty great, but I'm too tired to even mumble.

The benefits are strangely lasting, too. To Durancos's dog, Lander, attaining the summit of Gilbert Peak is unimportant. To Tee, Sean and I, it holds great value. We can never drive west across southwestern Wyoming on I-80 on a sunny day and not think of Lander and remember our grand day on Gilbert Peak, for Gilbert on a clear day is impossible to miss.

And in the end, Gilbert proves to be a hinge. So great is our experience that we rededicate ourselves to the ruined red range. We seek to spend much Uinta time and effort. We will not let a year go by without at least trying one big trip to the heights and many other trips to the edges.

I thank the Great Spirit and all the Lucky Stars that we were up there together: myself and Blondie, Tee and Daisy, Sean McHelen, and especially Don Durancos's dog, Lander. *Long may you run, noble brother. Long may all of us run.*

Postscript: It turns out I was mistaken about Nathan Shoulders. He eventually finds a calling in exercise science and the martial arts. For a living he teaches classes at all levels and even enters the cage as a professional fighter. That all would have changed, of course, if he had gone up Gilbert Peak.

```
        M
        E
    M A N Y
        D
    M O O S E
        W
        S
```

Mt. Lovenia, part two

Tee Trundler and I go up the East Fork aiming for Lovenia in early June, 2001, and it is very wet. We see a lot of wildlife.

Because of an exceptionally early start, at the first stream crossing at first light, we see a couple of dozen elk, a bunch of bambi and a herd of moose—we count thirteen. Moose are often seen alone, in pairs or in a family group. This is the only time I've ever seen a herd. All day long we see more moose, at least one in every meadow. (This adventure is detailed in "The Longest Day," in *Big Wonderful.*)

After a lengthy approach, when we start up the face, I get the willies, bale, and once again sit and wonder. I dry my boots. I think about my young son, my wife, our kids, our responsibilities. I was just as chicken before I had these, though, so it doesn't really leave much of a way out. Maybe it's okay to know your limits.

Tee Trundler goes directly up the North-East face of Lovenia, one gully west from the top, up steep snow and rock. He notches the top and glissades the next gully west of the ascent route, completing it in a couple hours. This one-day solo ascent rates ultimo-gnar grade IV. The T. Trundler Direct erases any doubt about his preeminence as a mountaineer.

Then we walk back all the way out of the East Fork, trying really hard to stay together and not fall into a stream. We feel tired for several days afterward.

Tokeanother

Thirteen years after "The Slopes of Tokewanna," Tee and I come back to the West Fork to climb Tokeanother on the last day of June, with Sean and Larissa McHelen. At camp my lovely wife Jennifer stays with our wonderful son Christopher. They're okay with that, since Chris is six and Jennifer is smart. Everything is different. Nothing is the same.

Tee, Sean, Larissa and I take the revolting, trail-less, bushy, slippery, meandering, boulder-bloated side canyon to the upper basin and then bear right rather than straight ahead. There's quite a bit of snow in fields on the freeze-thaw. We climb Tokeanother on that snow, in insistent wind, and there are no clouds in the sky.

I look over at Tokewanna a couple of times and try not to. It remains a huge-ass malevolent rusty slag pile of a peak. Repellent, really.

Sometimes I want to steer my son from wanting to climb peaks for the very reason that there are places such as that and days such as those. He's probably got no interest, though, sign of better sense.

But for you, Dear Reader? Who can say, really? Your daughter, friends, spousal unit? Or anyone? Would you want them to have at the Toke with or without you?

Still and all, you've got to know the dark to know the light, or to put it more empirically, you get to know the dark to know the light. You must pay with Tokewanna for a perfect day somewhere else. [Insert name of fine ascent.] There is much to like up here. Such places are good in your mind and in your future. Give into it. Get out there.

Tokewanna is good to have done. Had it not been done, its being undone would still cause sorrow. Tokewanna, Tokeanother, Wasatch—all three taken care of, and the world better because of it. The whole high long crazy ridge, done to perfection.

Thirteen years. The same and a different me. A different day, different route. Even the Toke had changed.

You never climb the same mountain twice.

Rip

In a long ramble of the kind on a fine autumnal day, Rip had unconsciously scrambled to one of the highest parts of the Kaatskill mountains...
— Washington Irving, 1819

In the off season we look at maps. Snowed out of the highest country, we make plans for the next season, or the seasons after that. Most of these plans involve a lot more talking than action. Some of them are pipe dreams. Some of them quite plainly ridiculous.

Invariably when Sean is visiting me or I am visiting him, at some late point in the evening, we'll spread the maps out and begin a lot of hot and empty big talking. We generally like to make sure that Larissa is near. Within ten minutes of the beginning of our seminar, she will be stretched out on a nearby sofa gathering then sawing logs.

We do not unfurl our maps in my lovely Jennifer's presence. No, she would denigrate our activity and place unfavorable words including "stupid," "pointless," "really?" and "here we go again," if we did.

For added style points, we never consult a guidebook for the Uintas, just maps. We have grown familiar with the range and would feel somehow cheated if we looked to someone else for advice or accept someone else's lame names for good names. Granted, maps don't show routes like guidebooks do, and maps also might get a person into trouble, but hey, it's a risk worth taking. Also, there are dozens of potential routes on any given Uinta peak. Surely normal routes exist, but there's no need for any intimate description beyond "west ridge" or "northwest face." Look at a map, look at a peak, and figure out a way.

Wilson Peak is the highest peak in Utah no one ever sees. Viewed from the north, it is hidden behind its more showy neighbors and hard to make out. From the south, it can be seen only from a couple of places in the Uintah Basin. From the east and west, forget it. This situation gives Wilson its particular charm. From its summit perhaps the finest view in the Uintas may be had, precisely because Wilson (named for another science guy) is right in the middle of things.

"Kevin, how can you say that it has the finest view? What on earth are your criteria?"

Scrambling High Unita Peaks

Just trust me on this one, judge the book by its cover. But sure, assessing the quality of a mountain's view may seem somewhat subjective. For one, it's dependent on ever-changing atmospheric conditions. When a peak is obscured by clouds or mists or rain or hail, it would be impossible to praise the view, for there is none. Views from the tops of mountains are also more or less the same: rocks, ridges, glaciers, cliffs, boulder fields, moraines, lakes, forests, lowlands — if you've seen one, you've seen them all.

Getting back to Wilson: the view from the top is very fine for several reasons. The actual summit is flat and good-sized. No hateful false summits mar the ascent. From the summit platform many pretty lakes mirror the sky. On the north side a yawning red gulf falls away. To the east the whole Gunsight to Powell ridge-o-rama stretches in candy-apple red, and there's a whole lot of it. It contrasts very effectively with the blue-green lakes of the upper Red Castle, the green-black forests below and the blue-gray-dun Bridger Valley beyond.

Red Castle itself looms in layers, looking like a gigantic red castle. Nor is the southern sweep something you have to put a paper bag over. Over on the left stand Kings and South Kings, and there's no doubt that they stand regal with vast gully-runnelled western faces. On the back side, the long curve of the Mellowstone River stretches and spills all the way down to the low country.

Yes, Wilson Peak is right in the middle of the big stuff: from Tokewanna to Gilbert to Emmons, Utah's pilasters are laid out for anyone to see.

Except for a miserable schisty stretch and a dollop of semi-steep snow, the route Tee, Sean and

I take up Wilson is free of challenging impediments and bad talus. The only trouble, and the saving grace of this hill is that it lies fifteen miles from the nearest trailhead, although it seems quite a bit farther in than that. In fact, it seems about twenty years in.

Tee Trundler, Sean McHelen and I are middle-aged humans. This is a working vacation for us. Unlike Rip van Winkle, who prefers the profession of idleness, we are gainfully employed, contributing to our country and communities, and this sojourn is a way to get away.

Tee and Sean are both weekend warriors, though, active outdoorsy types. Trundler put in 101 Wasatch ski days last season, while holding down a "real" job. A hundred and one ski days is obsessive and excessive, shows a lack of family responsibilities, was probably way too much fun, and makes me very jealous. On the other hand, getting that far out may be a problem down the slope.

Sean is a few years younger but no longer a *poulet de printemps*. His form of aerobic punishment has two wheels. He likes to ride his bicycle many dozens of miles. Each September, together with hundreds of other misguided souls, he peddles a two-wheeler from Logan, Utah to Jackson, Wyoming, some 212 miles, and considers this to be fun. Sean has no children yet and a younger wife.

Me, I'm on the flabby middle-aged white-guy end of the spectrum. My daily life is contemplative rather than active. I'm prone to melancholy and indolence. Often I drive a computer. I can't keep up with Tee or Sean and don't really try to. They'll

wait for me, eventually. I've got various excuses for
my less-than-ideal physical condition, some good,
others not, but with my inner strength and fortitude,
I find I can still go along for the ride because it's
good clean fun. I walk alone, I walk alone.

*From an opening…he could overlook all
the lower country for many a mile…*

Our present system is not devoted to zero-
impact camping, self-abnegation and asceticism.
Seasons in the past were, and many were the dues
paid in purity and lesser impacts, when one trod the
moral high ground, following zero-impact style and
clinging to techniques designed to leave no trace.

To mention one, yea verily, in my salad days
I eschewed even a teeny twig fire. No build no fire,
young man. I didn't build no fire, never.

I humped a bulging backpack and cast
aspersions upon those who rode upon the backs of
four-legged beasts, or who used such beasts to carry
their larder. I did little to stimulate the economy
of the United States of America. I owned less than
one vehicle and no domicile; had neither spouse
nor offspring; walked, used public transportation
and even peddled a bicycle; and in short enjoyed
the manifold blessings of a small carbon footprint,
basking in the faint green glow of eco-righteousness.
Nowhere was my carbon footprint smaller than in
the high ranges.

As a general principle it can be said that
knowing the dark side enables one to better know
the light. This is why some of the greatest saints

were sinners first. You can name several examples, certainly.

In fact, Rip, on this trip we've hired mules to carry in our gear. Mules! Lots of 'em. We've brought ample supplies to meet our needs for food and drink. We plan to build modest fires for entertainment and to keep us warm. We may bellow from the mountaintops. Portable music will lighten up our dark hours. Our domestic dogs will have the run of camp and chase o'er friendly sheep away.

We justify this because of our advanced ages, as a support of the undiversified Wyoming economy, because we have jobs now and have done it the other way, and because when it really comes right down to it, we probably don't have to justify it. It's a free country, even in Wyotah, and here's to it!

Say what you will, a nice docile mule is less intrusive than a troop of Boy Scouts, an ecclesiastical gathering, or a float in the parade of the world class.

Mules are far less invasive than sheep or cows. They earn their keep. The particular beauty of mules is simple: using them saves at least one day of hiking and quite a bit of pain and suffering because mules carry 150 pounds on their backs in panniers and you don't.

Fully laden, an old-style backpacker will find six/seven miles a day to be ample work. Eight/nine miles with some elevation gain is close to the limit. Also, while it is possible to carry more and go farther—to slay oneself in one massive day of painful, regrettable slog, it is not a pace that can be maintained. No, four-and-a-half to six hours of labor is the maximum that can be sustained day after day, at least for middle-aged American males and females.

Scrambling High Unita Peaks

What is the allure of the so-called through hiking? Just walking on a trail from dawn to dusk as far and as fast as you can? What sort of twisted Puritanical mojo got hold of you, Scorecard Monger?

The point of wilderness adventure is (or should be) what you do besides the walking or, to put it more delicately, beside the walking. In addition to the walking. You walk that you may also be idle beside a brook. You walk so you may also KWB — Kick Way Back and enjoy it.

Carrying a light day pack, though, with a friendly and attractive mule hauling your business, it is no great shakes to cover twelve miles — even with plenty of ups and downs — or fifteen, and to arrive at a destination without undue suffering: to arrive with eagerness to sample the accumulated pile of goodies hauled by the four-legged friends. Indeed, following such a "light" day in, the next day may even be a "summit" day, not a day of penance devoted to pain relievers and sanding of one's beveled edges.

On this particular trip we make it a point not to overdo it. We've kept our gear needs under control. We've had the mules carry an adequate amount of food. More important, we only bring in four cases of beer, some whiskey, and a responsible amount of wine.

Panting and fatigued, he threw himself, late in the afternoon, on a green knoll, covered with mountain herbage, that crowned the brow of a precipice.

RED STONE HEART

Moderation in everything, surely. Kenny, our muleteer, affirms that he has on occasion taken in pack trains with one, two, three, even four mules carrying the beer. But these were hunting trips, and hunters (all of whom are from out of state) like to imbibe to excess, and also, Kenny is prone to exaggeration. Kenny Aimone.

There lives a belt of Aimone's in this part of Wyoming. Kenny is one of the more colorful of the clan. He runs North Slope Outfitters and takes pack trains into the Uintas. Kenny is everything you might expect a horse and mule packer to be. He drives an ancient truck to pull a super-sized horse trailer. He knows all the drainages by heart and can give misleading information about any of them at the drop of an IFA hat. Kenny looks like an outfitter: reddish hair, blue-brown eyes, sun-blotched skin, barrel chest, pot belly. He wears a flannel shirt, wore-out Wranglers, dusty riding boots, topped off with a beat up cowboy hat. Kenny don't like to walk — that's what horses is for.

Kenny's job is to make people happy, to take them in to nice places with plenty of supplies for comfort. He knows, too, that part of his vocation is to dispense a little lore. As he is loading our canned barley pops onto one of the mules, he tells us that as high up as we were going, we'll just have to put 'em in the stream to keep 'em cold. Icy cold streams up there. Course, if there are snowdrifts, that'll be better.

We know that it has been an early summer. The snow is probably gone.

"That's how it was in Vietnam," he continues. "The soldiers would just put their beers in snowdrifts up there, then they'd turn them over eight times, and they'd be so cold, you couldn't hardly drink 'em."

"Eight times?" we ask, just to make sure.

Kenny nods.

"And this was over in Vietnam?"

"You bet. The soldiers just put their beers in the snowdrifts up there. Kept 'em so cold, you couldn't hardly drink 'em."

"Vietnam?"

"You bet. Brought them Buds in by helicopter."

Clearly this was something to look forward to.

As it turns out, camping at 10,700 feet, in a homespun site Kenny takes us to: a little shelf just above a little meadow with a little stream running through it has one further advantage, even without the snowdrifts of Vietnam: One's provisions stay cold naturally.

RED STONE HEART

As Tee, Sean and I have grown more advanced in years, we have embraced rest days. After, let us say, the chronological age of thirty-five or thirty-nine or forty-four, the human loses some resiliency and strength. To perform well requires some time off, some resting. This Rip van Winkle understands. Rip takes time off to consider the propositions. Rip takes a really long rest.

He doesn't fight it. He gives in to the imperative of R and R. And in the Catskill autumn, given certain circumstances, how would be it possible not to?

Rest days take a fair amount of effort. To rest and loiter, to linger and malinger, to force one's self to practice not doing is itself an effort. You must not do in order to do. Think in terms of the whole trip; Any ninny can overdo it so much for the first two or three days that the rest of the trip is a chore. This is what dogs nearly always do, wearing themselves out in pointless, tiresome games. But with the holistic view: if you spend one-third or one-quarter of the time seriously devoted to resting, the rest of the trip will be more enjoyable.

It is a generally a good idea to establish an agenda for the rest day, even if it is to establish no agenda (establishing an agenda or not in a meaningful way takes work, and discussion). Approving an agenda, or the consideration of having no agenda, requires following Robert's Rules of Order and a good deal of palaver. In all things good planning nets good results.

For instance, it's a good idea to pencil in some type of rest day activity: stately picnic, sightseeing at a select locale, bird watching in yonder willow stand, exploring the pretty little meadow just over there and nothing more (to maximize results.)

To speak personally, I've found one of the best sporting rest day activities is fishing or not fishing. Fishing or not fishing gives you something to build around, to work toward, to fill up the lazy hours.

It's possible to fish and not fish in the same day. While some members of a party fish, others will not fish, again maximizing happiness.

In addition to making an agenda, it's a good idea to continuously monitor it for quality control. Getting behind schedule is perfectly allowable. Indeed, it can be a prelude to jettisoning the agenda altogether, often a good idea right around lunch time.

Here's a sample working template for a good rest day:

7:00-9:00 a.m.	Breakfast, ablutions.
9:00-10:00 a.m.	Walk slowly to lake or stream for observation.
10:00-noon	Fish, not fish.
12:00-2:00 p.m.	Lunch (can be extended).
2:00-4:00 p.m.	Fish, not fish.
4:00-5:00 p.m.	Walk slowly back to camp.
5:00-7:00 p.m.	Sumptuous dinner.
7:00-8:00 p.m.	Talk about feelings.
8:00-10:00 p.m.	Fire and radio time.

To join together in planning such an agenda increases the sense of commitment and solidarity. Keep in mind that angling (or not) here is simply a generic. Virtually anything productive may be substituted: sketching, reciting poetry, bird watching, examining boulders, botanizing, making lists, playing small musical instruments, pressing wildflowers, singing, using your atlatl and/ or examining philosophical or religious questions.

What if the weather turns bad?

Got it covered. Find some trees or a cave, bring an ultra-light tarp.

What if the fishing stinks?

Try not fishing.

What if lunch takes more than two hours?

Good on ya, mates!

What if you never make it but a hundred paces from camp?

Savor those hundred paces.

At the end of such a well-structured rest day, who could say nothing valuable was accomplished?

Compare "And we like walked a helluva long way, Dude" to "Much have I traveled in this four-acre meadow." It is no contest in terms of enlightenment.

Walking on rest days is something to be careful about. Do not overdo it. It is possible, and should be, to stretch crossing a meadow into an hour's progress. At any time during a rest day, if a view of wild animal, or a bend in the stream, or a particularly lovely clutch of marsh orchids, or a picturesque rock outcropping, or the perfect arrangement of bank, stream and russet willow — if anything should demand your attention, then by all means stop: attend to it, study it, contemplate it, photograph it, embrace it, relish it.

A seasoned camper will bring a small, lightweight sitting pad or chair on all such journeys. The pad or chair has several virtues: it insulates the buttock from the cold, provides comfort for sore body parts down there, delineates personal space choices at the camping site or out and about — this here's mine/you may sit over there—and provides that extra measure of comfort when one's back is softly resting against a tree or rock. A padded seat and back support makes resting a real pleasure, particularly when potables and viands are spread about, and the scene is grand and unfolding.

When out and about on a rest day, don't hesitate to plop that sitting pad or chair down. Just up and plop it down and proclaim a halt. Halt here and now. Good things are sure to follow.

Fishing can be a problem in this regard. Too often the angler longs to feel the tug the fin-bearing denizens of the deep and overdoes it, thrashing through stands of willow, clambering over rocks, and slipping into beaver trenches, while roving from hole to hole. It can be a challenge to cast a fly while sitting. In this way the spinning rig is superior: one can cast the spinner quite effectively while seated. Just pretend that shoreline boulders are seats in a boat, and you'll get the hang of it pretty quickly. Standing and roving takes more energy than sitting.

Scorecard mountaineers and stopwatch climbers are often rightly criticized for being so focused on the goal that all else is shut out, passed by in a hurry, not seen. There may be some truth to this charge. In the end, does it matter if you made it to the top in three hours, thirty-five minutes and fourteen seconds if you didn't see anything along the way?

Yes, actually it does.

The reality map of the high mountains demands both strenuous labor and leisure time.

RED STONE HEART

One works best with the other, as in complimentary flavors. To fully appreciate the rest day, you need to make yourself very tired, which isn't difficult.

Again, moderation in everything, surely. I'd prefer to be moderate in most things but to be deliciously excessive about a few choice things. This brings us to *Fajitas de las Truchas*.

The secret to good-tasting fish is freshness. This is certainly true of the wily mountain trout, and indeed the high mountain angler can avail herself of trout in the very pink of freshness, straight from the lake or stream. It's minutes from stream to skillet, seconds under the right circumstances. That's hours—or days—faster than Tsukiji or Pike's Place, friends.

Once the decision is made to keep a trout, it ought to be slain and cleaned as soon as possible. The prep is simple and direct on the mountain trout: chop, slice, pull, and at ten thousand feet, the coolness of the ambient air allows a prepared trout to be stored for hours in the cool of one's backpack, creel or man purse.

Catching two or three trout for dinner should be an uncomplicated matter. When the angling is good, it's often very good. At times the mountain trout practically beg to be caught. When you prefer to release your fish, the same haste should be practiced: get that speckled, darting beauty back into the water just as quickly as you can. Release it, thank it for its service, and try not to catch it again.

There are two good-tasting ways to prepare trout. The old fashioned way is pan frying over a camp stove or fire. Fry 'em in bacon grease if you can. Don't forget the spices. It's really messy and smelly (a potential problem in bear country) but it's done right in front of your eyes, and it certainly makes the skin taste better. A lightly browned, well-seasoned fresh-fried trout is delish. Good, lightweight frying pans are widely available. If you cook over a fire, though, the pan will be ruined.

The other method uses aluminum foil and coals. The technique is simple: Trout are arranged and prepared in a little foil boat. Coat all sides of the fish with a dollop of fat (margarine, butter or oil). Add spices: lemon pepper, sage, onion flakes, garlic salt, whatever you have brought along (and be sure you bring some along). Then simply seal the foil boat up, add another layer of foil to prevent leakage, and place it on the shimmering coals. This is the preferred way for *Fajitas de las Truchas*.

Since most people don't like bones, you need to fillet the trout after cooking, which is simple. Just slice along the backbone, gently separate each side of flesh, pull the backbone free, and toss it in the fire. It may be necessary to pluck out a fin or two, but the whole process can be done quickly and with little mess. Nestle a few trout fillets on a bed of rice, garnish with a sprig of dill or sage, and season with a squeeze of lemon and/or a dollop of hot sauce, and you will not feel cheated.

If you have time and inclination, though, you should make up a mess of fish fajitas.

Find a flat rock or a large log upon which to work. While the fish is cooking, as above, you have about an hour to assemble the rest of the ingredients.

Each member of a group should bring a small vial of hot sauce, and try to make sure you bring different brands. Hot sauce is repackaged into little screw cap bottles that weigh next to nothing. A few drops go a long way, adding zest to any humble gruel. Remember some lime or lemon juice; again, a little does a lot. Also, you need to bring a small can of salsa. These are available in green, red, ranchero or picante. The weight-conscious may want to use dehydrated salsa. You'll use the salsa in everything, including as a dip for the tube of chips that someone just opened. Tubed chips may not be one's first choice, but they will not get crushed, and they come in a variety of fairly edible flavors.

While the fish is gently baking on the coals and the chips and salsa are out and about, it would be a good time to find a Latin station on the radio, and also a good time to drink some tequila. If you have mules, then you brought some pre-mixed margaritas, or some lemon-lime sports drinks, and you have mixed the tequila thereunto to make a pitcher of "Gatoritas." If you are really lucky (or are in Vietnam) you have found a snow bank, and the ice crystals softly swirling in the swill make drinking easy. Also, you may find that after a point, tequila works well when chased with Mexican beer. Leading brands are available in cans.

If, on the other hand, you have had to carry all this in on your back, you can make surprisingly drinkable swill using a powdered drink mix (lemon lime), or simply chug-a-lug with a little salt on your hand. Nor would it be the wrong time to pop the cork on a box of stout red wine and pass around goblets.

During this time, you'll need to do a little cooking. First, make some rice. The various mixes are fine: dirty rice, Spanish rice, Mexican rice, even white or brown rice with some dribbles of lime and hot sauce.

Next, make up a pot of instant black or pinto beans. Add a little extra water, a spritz of lime, and set the rice and beans near the fire so they will stay warm. Don't forget to add some cheese on top. Since you remembered to bring onion and tomatoes (Romas keep well), you'll want to dice these now and slice and deploy the bell peppers or jalapeños.

Someone will have to cut the cheese and also arrange the few sprigs of cilantro. Flour tortillas are the best choice for backpacking. Sandwich a package between a few paper plates and you can protect the tortillas and have something clean to eat them on.

Once the trout are done, the final steps require the division of labor. Someone needs to warm the tortillas either on a clean flat rock, a portable grill, or in aluminum foil. If someone did bring a grill, then by all means make a quesadilla or three for one of your first courses: in time, you'll figure out how much fire will melt the cheese and brown but not burn the tortillas. Someone else should check on the rice, beans, and make sure everyone's goblets are full. Someone else needs to deal with the trout.

Fillet the trout and remove all the fins, as above. Also, carefully separate the flesh from the skin. In a clean bowl gently toss the flaked trout chunks with lime, cilantro and salsa. Now you are ready. Place all the dishes and all the condiments together on the flat rock or large rock. Give thanks to the Great Spirit. Pile all on a tortilla and roll it up. Dig in! Repeat. Repeat.

This is one of the best ways to spend two or three hours on a rest day. Or four. We've all got to eat. Might as well eat well. Rice, beans, tortillas, trout, spices, peppers, queso, salsa, tomatoes, onions — *c'est bon.*

In terms of wilderness camping, fire has two sides. One side holds that fire is a violation of zero-impact philosophy. Fires — even modest fires — make smoke, use up nutrients, leave some waste behind, and given modern gear, are unnecessary. In heavily used areas, they are illegal. In many areas, they are wrong: near timberline, by popular lakes, in most national parks, and so on. Wrong! Untended campfires cause forest fires every summer. And let's not even get started on global warming. Build not fire, young person.

This was a creed I lived by for many years and often stood smug and sweet smelling as I traversed the rock-rich boulder fields to the moral high ground.

Later, as I underwent changes, I went over to the other side. The dark bright side. At this time

Scrambling High Unita Peaks

I cannot relate when the change occurred, for the story of the incident with the spruce and the baby doll is so plainly embarrassing that, well…someday, I may perhaps share it with the public (even though it poses a legitimate threat to my Senatorial ambitions). But at this juncture let me simply confess that I went over to the other side and now build fires seldom but freely.

Not everywhere, mind you. And never in the high season. Maybe not in town. But in the colder months, in thick forests and away from the maddening crowds, I honor our shared heritage with fire. A large part of camping has to do with sitting and staring at a fire.

With fire there's the burning fire and the unburning fire, the ashes and the flame. In much of the Rockies these days, with so many stands of trees dead from the climate change and bark beetles, it may be that a few conservative campfires help rather than harm forest health by taking care of excess deadfall. But let's watch the wind, the timber load and humidity. To look at the sorry state of western forests, there are going to be some huge wildfires during the next decades of the change.

Fire is one of the deepest and most primal pleasures in camping. Just why this is so is not hard to determine. Fire provides warmth, light, a focal point for gathering, cheer, smoke, protection from wild animals, a way to cook, something to do during the dark and cold hours—a highly human thing to experience. When the flames have died down and only the coals remain shifting brightly in the evening breeze, the orange glowing mirror of summers past displays the spiritual/mortality element better than anything else.

RED STONE HEART

One wonders what our distant ancestors did before fire. How did they fill their nights? Probably by dreaming of fire, or something like fire. Something to gather 'round for warmth, comradery. A parish church under the open sky.

Winter, as well as early or late season camping, would be less comfortable without a meaningful bit of burning. There's just something about fire in the snow that makes sense, a way of beating back the natural surge.

In the backcountry fire pits can become a real problem and create obvious impacts in highly-used areas. Inexplicably, one often finds five or six fire rings at the same campsite, and there's no real way to justify that. Another problem with fire pits is that stupid and careless people seem to think they are waste repositories, and so they toss whatever they don't want to carry in there, making a litter-magnet eyesore. Fire rings invite camping and impact.

The old and valid advice about backcountry camping is that if you chose to build a fire, use an existing ring. Never make a new one. Where there is no ring or rocks, go without. If you must make a ring, dismantle it after use: toss the rocks and scatter the ashes. (You can purchase reusable portable fire rings and bring them along.) Some common sense, too, can be applied to firewood gathering: Standing or fallen dead, only—you should be able to break it off with your hands.

Some planning and research, though, can make having a fire no worse than anything else you do: driving your car to the trailhead, paying taxes, shopping at Walmart. Pick an area of heavy vegetation—look at a topo map. Also, try to camp away from places of obviously heavy use.

Scrambling High Unita Peaks

Another element of less-than-zero impact is called a portable musical device. These ingenious little devils weigh only a couple of ounces. You can even get solar powered ones. They are so small the noise they make can scarcely be heard a few feet away.

Why bring a portable radio or i-pad with speakers? Because in many areas of the mountain world, depending on the season, it gets dark by five p.m. or six or seven or eight, leaving many (too many) hours of darkness with nothing much to do. Some people bring books and read them in their tents. That works with some people and some tents. To speak frankly, my one-person tent is so small that to try to slither into it and do anything other than sleep is pure misery. Even with a big tent, go to sleep at eightish and you'll be ready and raring to go at three am, and that's sure no fun unless it's a summit day.

No, we've developed a strategy to cope with staying up late. It's called building a fire, listening to the radio, and playing silly games such as calling out which awful band from one's teenage years will be played next on the classic hits, whether the song will be good or suck, whether the artist will be male or female, or if you prefer country, whether the song will be about drankin', Daddy, Mama, fidelity/ infidelity or nostalgia. AM radio can be illuminating too, especially after dark, when you can pick up odd bits and pieces from all over the world.

Speaking of morning, Jennifer claims that I don't like to get up early and won't "unless you're climbing some stupid mountain." There's a kernel of veracity there. Getting out of bed before Aurora leaves her bed is not something I prefer to practice; it puts me in a foul and unfriendly mood. You didn't ask, but I'm not the kind of person who can sleep-in either, I simply prefer to start the day in the light rather than the dark. Call me a wimp, but call me after 9:00 a.m.

When it comes to mountaineering, though, experience teaches the necessity of the early start. There are two reasons for this: weather and the long day's labor. In greener days, as we have seen, I had the bad habit of getting to the top right about 1:00 p.m., a time which coincided with the daily onset of electrical activity. After doing this a few times, I grew to understand that it would be better to get closer to the base of the climb the day before, when practicable, and also to start as early as possible.

Again, there ought to be moderation in everything. Starting in the dark in the High Uintas backcountry might well result in getting lost, as there are often few trails and very thick trees. The summit bid begins at the campsite and usually off trail. It is enough to be ready, tuned up and rocking by 5:30-6:00 a.m. 6:30 a.m. can work. 7:00 a.m. is late, so hurry.

First light is right.

This schedule provides room for several hours of intense activity, while you're still fresh, and time to get up and off the top before the hair-raising crackling begins. Afternoons can thus be reserved for the lollygag, either with many stops along the way, or a quick return to camp and its amenities.

Too, these quiet frosty early morning hours

are the best times to see wildlife up close, and one can seem to cover more ground before the sun is risen high. One's Puritan roots demand some type of labor, after all. One does not enter the kingdom of heaven without good works and without sacrifice.

For some time Rip lay musing on this scene; evening was gradually advancing; the mountains began to throw their long blue shadows over the valleys; he saw that it would be dark long before he could reach the village, and he heaved a heavy sigh when he thought of encountering the terrors of Dame Van Winkle.

I love my wife. Her name is Jennifer Sorensen. She's a fiery one, strong as rock and tough as iron. A college professor and often fun, she's a talented, enterprising woman who puts up with my mood swings and work habits despite her better sense, to say nothing of her generosity, loyalty and inner and outer beauty.

I also love, though naturally to a lesser extent, Tee's wife, Lady Trundler and Sean's wife, Larissa. I love them all and love that they are not here. I would not intimate disrespect in this connection. Many are the trips we take together. We purchase them a lodge and present them trinkets to show loyalty and receive favor.

I mean nothing but adoration here, either: but these long glorious days are significantly better because our wives are not here. Not just different, but better. If they were here, our feelings and experiences would be deeper, surely, and our perceptions clearer, and our conversation full of more topics than elimination processes and routes up peaks. But it would be different.

Now, I'm the last one to say that women are not the equals of men. Hell no. Witness a childbirth and you will learn that men are weaklings, wimps. Regarding my male friends, many of whom are quite strong and very fit, not one of them would be able to give birth to another human. No, he'd feign dizziness, or complain about his tendonitis or bunions, or he'd get someone else to do it for him, he'd say he wasn't comfortable at the sight of blood.

The women are stronger. Our little women know this and let us come out here to play, without them, because all this ensures domestic tranquility. A division of labor is a good thing. We take mancations, they have womencations, and all is well with the world.

Freedom and bondage work well together, in moderation. This Rip Van Winkle also knew. Rules are good. Good too are no rules.

That's nice, but maybe someday I'll only have my wonderful better half with whom to adventure and time to institute a different style of wilderness exploration.

On the summit day whoever is up first needs to make as much noise as possible while starting the chores. Starting the chores has obvious benefits, making plentiful noise has a purpose too.

If you happen to be the first one out of the tent or tarp, many are the sparkles. There is the moral high ground for being the first one up, the earliest to rise. First up lasts all day. There is the magical time before first light. Magically cold as well as magically dark. Soon the sky will faintly lighten around the edges. The day's first robin sings. Greet the happy, sing-song bird with a brisk "hallo" of rocks. Just one happy little robin. A little noise will also frighten the gathered, teeming bears away.

Stumble over to the fire ring. Hands too cold for much intricate work. Pluck up a large red-needled bough, brought in the night before, touch it with a lighter, and presto, instant fire. Noisily break a few branches to toss onto the cheery orange sparking, popping flames.

Do the no-good companions yet rustle? They do not. Only the blessed robins — now a pair.

Might was well start the stove. Since you are well prepared, you fetched a pail of water the night before. Soon pot is on the flame, and soon the dark celestial elixir will begin coursing down the gullet. They can start their own darned stoves.

Consider your efforts. Just barely enough photons to make out more than shadows. The fire is happily crackling. The stove is purring. The arrowing pines surround you as ancestors and powerful beings. This is good medicine. You packed your summit pack and pumped or purified two quarts last night. No annoying fumbling for whatnot, no leaving something behind. Embrace the moral high ground. Just about ready to go.

It's 5:27 a.m. in the Mountain West. Shout about it. Break some more branches. Toss another rock or two. Shout, "Oh no, it's a bear, and…it's charging!" That'll wake the dreamers.

Hot drinks, oatmeal — perform the morning ablutions, and you'll be on your way.

RED STONE HEART

By degrees Rip's awe and apprehension subsided. He even ventured, when no eye was fixed upon him, to taste the beverage, which he found had much of the flavor of excellent Hollands. He was naturally a thirsty soul, and was soon tempted to repeat the draught.

After a rough and tumble day out slogging peaks or blithely angling for the wily mountain trout, the consumption of a few canned barley sodas in quick succession in the late afternoon can be an intensely pleasurable experience to those who are that way inclined. It has been said that intense physical exertion at altitude increases one's susceptibility to Bacchanalian delights. Rip van Winkle knew this well, even at the puny heights of the Catskills. Weight is a consideration. Many drinkable wines are available in boxes. Some good mellow wine can provide a *bella sera*, all things considered.

Wine is fine; ales are also good for what ails you. Cheap American beer in patriotic cans can also soothe the weary. You got a problem with that? Many hoppy, roasted, infused or foo-foo craft ales, lagers and porters are available in cans.

Don't overlook a good aperitif or digestif: simply repackage your favorites in small screw-topped plastic bottles. Coffee-based liquor is a must, and don't forget the peppermint schnapps for cocoa, the Drambuie for love, a little Pernod if you've got the Van Gogh thing going on, and Courvoisier if your hip-hop friends are going to be dropping in.

Scrambling High Unita Peaks

Yet our camp is not on any trail. Although Kenny Aimone affirms that we are fifteen to eighteen miles from the trailhead, we know we are not, not quite. But we know we are so far in we will be left unmolested. In fact, during the twenty years we spend at our campsite, we only see two people; both are soloists, and one a moron.

The first person we encounter is a lanky young individual at Smiths Fork Pass. Returning from Wilson Peak, we're lunching at the pass when this darkly bearded twenty-five year old guy walks up. He stops and chats.

A Forest Service volunteer, he is likely headed back to graduate school at CSU or USU or MSU or NAU in the fall. For fun during his summer job, on his days off he goes for really long hikes. Already fourteen miles into it, he will traverse the upper Yellowstone, scramble up Anderson Pass and spend the night up there, probably sleeping higher than anyone in Utah. In the morning he'll probably knock of Kings before walking out the Henrys Fork. He's carrying a well-used frame pack that is under-stuffed. His clothes are neither sporty, stylish nor in very good repair. His boots are trashed. He knows where he is, what he's doing, and where he is headed. He is headed for solitary glory.

Granted, he does not grasp just how important Wilson Peak is to us, nor does he ask for our autographs, but he doesn't speak any more than necessary. A humble soloist in the prime of youthful adventure and glory.

There is some hope for the youth of this great

country! Lunch done, we salute him as we walk away the other way and later toast him with Fosters oil cans we had left in a snowbank just below the pass. To speak truly, several hours in a snowbank made the ale quite cold and yet quite easy to drink. Special bitter it is, and we are not.

From looking at maps during the winter, I know there's a gully that leads from Smiths Fork up to Flat Top, and from Flat Top it's a short way to Mount Powell. At our camp, we are able to see the bottom of this gully.

The combination of fish fajitas, a bracing and well-colored sunset, and the fact that we have no desire to go back up to Smiths Fork Pass, combine to give glowing inspiration for the route to Mount Powell.

We will take the gully up to Flat Top, and who knows, maybe there is grass rather than talus up there, and then we'll simply walk the not-so-very steep ridge presently towering above us to the top of Powell, also presently towering above us. We will do this in the morning. It will be a good thing to do, much better than the route suggested in Tee's odious guidebook. Plus, the most northerly of Powell's three summits, the one closest to us, is the highest.

Mount Powell is named in honor of John Wesley Powell, the well-known explorer of the Green and Colorado Rivers, founder of government bureaus, associate of the wealthy and powerful. Major Powell, who lost his right arm at the battle of Shiloh, remains as a larger-than-life figure in the West. Powell wrote a sensational and popular memoir about his journey down the Colorado, where he combines two different expeditions into one. He also penned an indispensable treatise about water, land, irrigation, and agriculture in our region. One would not, however, have wanted to be one of Major Powell's crew, especially not on the first voyage.

Having said that, the solely-south-pawed major is certainly honored by Mount Powell, for it is one of the wonders of the Uintas. Its three summits are laid out as a mile-long ridge and form the high western rampart of the red and rearing Henry's Fork-Smiths Fork extravaganza.

Flat Top itself is a grassy marvel, just rotten with prime elk habitat. And indeed we see some elk, running north, away from unexpected visitors. Along the way, facing northeast and spilling down into Henry's Fork, we find what has to be the finest wilderness giant slalom pitch in Utah, if not the world, perfectly wide and perfectly steep. We vow to try it.

So warm is the summit dome that we don't touch a sweater or jacket but sit upon conglomerate and schist and bask in midmorning glory 12,692 feet up.

Half-an-hour up low-angled Death Platters and we're on top of Powell before 11:00 a.m. Would that all Uinta peaks give themselves so easily! Sean's dog Maggie knocks off the other two, lower summits, so we don't have to.

RED STONE HEART

Back down on earth, toward sunset, we sit in our little campsite meadow and gaze upon the ruddy slopes of the vanquished peak. We toast ourselves. We toast Major Powell. We enjoy cigars brought just for the occasion. We toast our mules. We toast Rip van Winkle and Washington Irving. We toast Kenny Aimone. We toast the puny heights of the Catskills.

Walking up the trail across the way, a solo pilgrim salutes us with a bold "hello" and approaches. He's traveling ultra-light and ultra-clueless. He's not sure where he's at and wonders if we can help him. He'd gotten lost in the lower Henry's Fork, taken a wrong turn, taken two more, and then finds himself a whole drainage over from where he thought he was, or so he thinks he thinks. "So like, this is Smiths Fork, right?" He is of the tribe and inclination of Dumbass, Shirley.

We disclose his actual location, point with pride at Mount Powell, and in answer to his most pressing question, we urge him to get-along-little-doggie up the trail another half hour before it's dark. Once we mention Lake So-and-So, he's suddenly quite intent on reaching it, which is good.

"And do for sure carry on! You're almost there." We assure him once again: "It's only ten or fifteen minutes, Bro."

He's carrying all the latest go-light through-hiker gear, and we wink as we watch him walk away, onward and upward, hoping he won't return. He was lost and now we helped him on his way. We were not about to share potables, viands or smoke with him, the bloody idiot. Wasn't even sure if he was in Smiths Fork?

In seeing him we try not to see ourselves. If we are honest, we have to admit that we have gotten badly lost many, many times, (maybe not that lost) and we too have been of the inclination of lost and lonely.

One taste provoked another; and he reiterated his visits to the flagon so often that at length his senses were overpowered, his eyes swam in his head, his head gradually declined, and he fell into a deep sleep.

Eventually, though, our idyll will be ended. From the mountaintop we have overlooked the changes on the world. We have played games in the meadow and by the fireside. We have stood upon the heights. We have quaffed draughts and spoken of our feelings. We have not been unhappy for some time away from our wonderful wives, those terrible viragos. We have disported with a few trout, rainbows that dance on the surface, brookies that pull the line to the deep, cutthroats with their gray-black pebbled sides, cruising like shadows at feeding time.

At length we will awaken again. We will go down, down to the valley below. Twenty years is a long, long time to be away.

The Ten Essentials

For a long day's journey:
    Day pack
    Water in container, water purification
    Food
    Duct tape
    Good pipes or a willingness to sing, holler,
    bellow, shout or speak loudly, or softly,
    depending
    Matches, lighter
    Hat, sunglasses, sunscreen
    Headlamp or flashlight[s], batteries
    Knife

Scrambling High Unita Peaks

Simple first-aid, repair supplies
A positive mental attitude
Emergency shelter: rain jacket, poncho
or tarp
Whistle, cell phone or walkie-talkie
Extra clothes
Oh, I almost forgot: Map and compass

For overnight add:
Sleeping bag, pad
Spirit of teamwork and cooperative problem
solving
Stove, fuel, cooking pot, cup and spoon
Shelter: tent, tarp or cave
More food

Choose from the following toppings:
Insect deterrent and/or bear deterrent
Camera
Sketchbook, notebook, guidebook, book,
scripture
Poles, walking stick or cane
Ice axe
Special boots
Skis
Snowshoes
Snowboard
Binoculars, monocular, spotting scope
Angling implements
Small musical instruments
Climbing rope and iron-mongery, crampons
Raft, pfd, pump, paddle
Atlatl

Part V
Island Wilderness

2005-2012

*Out here
the sky
palms aces.*

—Ken Brewer
Lake's Edge

Scrambling High Unita Peaks

Wheelbarrow Ridge

Early season, South Slope.

Not to be in a rush, but I'd like to take this opportunity to introduce my thirty-eight-pound backpack. What's that? Not good at introductions? Hey, don't run away just yet. No, of course I'm not going to ask you carry it. It's pretty light, though, for an expedition backpack.

Let me explain. This stuffed nylon pack bag, with the shoulder straps and not-very-comfortable padded hip belt, contains everything I will need for the next four or five days. Well, not everything I need, but everything I need to use. The surroundings will furnish the other things I need. I mean, everything that we will need.

Oh, and by the way, four pounds of that weight is two quarts of water. A person has to drink, surely, and the more water you drink, the better you'll be. No reason for anxiety there, but toss that out, and there's only thirty-four pounds, and that includes about four pounds of backpack. Okay, now we're talking.

So, how do you wear it? You carry it on your back.

As I was saying, nothing extra here: just basic clothes, a tiny tent, a nice warm sleeping bag. It's June and we'll be sleeping at over eleven thousand feet. Food: the lightest available, as well as stove, first aid and survival stuff, and, yes, a little bit of fishing gear. I can't see any use for the ice axe, and that's already been left behind. You're okay with that?

The fishing gear is pared down, too. I decided to just go with a spinning rig, because it's easier to sit and toss a spinner when you're really tired. Ultra-light rod, ultra-light reel, a few swivels, six or so lures, a couple of sinkers, a stretch of line. That's it. No more than a pound and a half of angling essentials, closer to a pound.

I am not exaggerating. Of course I'll let you use it.

To be honest, I like to keep my fishing under control, and I don't like to not catch fish when I'm trying. In June, the ice has been off the lakes for only a few days. The trout should be easy to fool, if you catch my drift.

Look, there's tons of places to angle that you can drive to, or stop by after work, or perhaps even reach on a day hike, but the Chain Lakes are way beyond that. It would be wrong to come up here in June and eschew the angling. No, embrace it. It is good.

Sure, a person could go even lighter, but

I'm not into shivering up high or wearing the same tunic for the whole time, and I'm sure you'll agree. Everyone likes a Spartan smidgeon of comfort, and at my age, by Artemisia, I've earned it. No, those are surely your control issues, not mine.

What's that? You still don't want to carry it? You want me to carry it?

The trail's going to be flat for the first three miles. Sure you don't want to give it a try? Just for the first little bit? Hmmmm. Well, I'm not going to shoulder this stone until Tee and Sean show up. Well, okay. I'll rest and gather my inner strength.

Samuel Emmons was the cartographer on Clarence King's Survey of the Fortieth Parallel. He made the first fairly-reliable maps of the Uintas. To honor him, a lofty pile of rocks is called Mount Emmons, and that is our goal.

With or without maps, it is plain that there will be a lot of up on this trip. A lot of up and then some more up to reach the top of Emmons. The trail begins at sea level in the Uintas: eight thousand feet. Goodness, eight thousand feet is practically San Diego. Trailheads on the South Slope start low. Low!

The trail will follow Uinta Creek for three miles, then it will cross the creek and commence climbing. How much climbing? Over a vertical mile.

It would be unwise to carry an overdone load up that lengthy grade. That would be strenuous and difficult. With a relatively light pack, the way is still strenuous and difficult but somewhat less so.

When I was younger that amount of gain would have seemed something to scoff at. I am now forty-seven, though, and not exactly a paragon of fitness. Now I'm the scoffee, not the scoffer. I need every break I can get.

Tee Trundler and Stan McHelen arrive at the trailhead parking lot. My drive over from Wyoming was most vernal, I tell them, and they are glad to be out of Salt Lake. We dawdle, then regretfully shoulder packs for the journey. They have brought their dogs to carry a bit, but not much.

There's a dude ranch at the trailhead. The dude ranch's remuda of mules and horses, has been let into the canyon for the winter, since it's a natural pasture of great extent, guarded at the back with deep drifts and cliffs. We meet them on the trail, these horses and mules. They're half-wild from the winter, and they do not give way. They seem to have forgotten about people. They look at us shaggy and red-eyed and won't take no guano from nobody. Not today. Not ever. They hoof the ground, whinny, and will not move. They stand their ground, the remuda of Uinta Creek. No budge 'em. Horses and mules.

Indeed they threaten: "None shall pass…. We are the knights who say, Neigh."

Tee, Sean and I look at each other, bewildered. Wow, is this really happening? It sure seems real. But come on now….

It's three against a dozen. Then another dozen join the fray. The dogs don't help matters much, irritating rather than distracting the beasts.

"We are the knights who say, Neigh."

Drawing upon our years of experience and utilizing a no-huddle offense, with head fakes and look-over-here's, hut-hut, we toss rocks left to confuse and deceive them, then take to the brush and over boulders right to outflank 'em, and thrash through shrubbery to a meadowlet to get back on the trail beyond. It's hard work sprinting with our special backpacks.

They come after us, though. Several follow us up the trail, clip-clomping just a few steps behind, shadowing. It's unsettling. They're pushing it. They follow us almost all the way to the river bridge. Three miles is still three miles.

At the crossing, Sheep Bridge, we sheep pause to regain our strength and contemplate the hill. The remuda is gone, no help now.

Sean has brought the kitchen sink, as always, but only a stainless-steel one-bowler, an underpowered quarter-horsepower disposal as well, and sports only a plastic sprayer. He skipped the cast-iron double dipper he usually carries.

Tee Trundler's pack is svelte, like mine. Much pain have we shared in overcoming the overdo. Tee Trundler, an experienced seasoned veteran, the John Stockton of sloggers, crafty and consistent, always ready for assists and steals. Yet, still, there is a look of sullen horror in their eyes. Flat is back there. Hill is here.

The trail climbs and then it climbs some more. It also climbs. Long rocky switchbacks built for sheep and cattle and mules and horses. Rocky because there are just so many glacial-outwash stones about, rolled onto the trail to prevent erosion. A multitude of cobbles.

In the old days it must have been a regular feat to fight a zigzag up this hill. In fact, we see many old trails, now overgrown, as we ascend. East-southeast facing as it is, it loses snow fairly early, this slope. Certainly there were older trails, left by The People. As quiet and gigantic as it is, it feels as though this has been a thoroughfare for centuries.

I have seen Mt. Emmons many times but always from afar. While driving through the Uintah Basin it is possible to see the "Big E," snow-slobbered and imposing, for fifteen motoring miles or so, towering over bulked-up dark shoulders. Emmons is hidden from the north, revealed only from the tops of a few peaks and passes — a big round blob of a peak. We had seen it weirdly wintered from South Paul Knob just a couple months previously. Much different does it appear from different angles.

Still, in terms of the range it is an outlier, the most southern and eastern of the high peaks. Emmons is off by itself, pouting. Why? The fourth highest peak in the state, Emmons, is only four feet lower than Gilbert. Four feet! Could this be an injustice? Shoot dang, build a cairn, and they're equal.

Gilbert Peak, too, was named for a nineteenth century scientist, Grove Karl Gilbert, a tree-hugging man from birth. By all reports Samuel Emmons was a bedrock man of science. Rather than thinking of the "Big E" as four feet lower than the "Big G," I prefer to think of them as equals, separated by some few league's canvas of Painter Basin, drenched with high alpine artistry. How can four feet make one bronze and the other not bronze? Get one and receive a pass for the other. Let them share the bronze medal and light the fire within.

RED STONE HEART

We do not see Mt. Emmons on our journey today. We see the same old canyon scene getting smaller the higher we plod. It's a suspension of wishful thinking, a roadtrip. Tee and Sean are way ahead of me.

By the way, I have always imagined that Chain Lake Basin is verdant and green, rife with life, chock full of hummocks and swards, wildflowers and burbling streams, nymphs and fauns. I think about these pictures under the duress of the ascent.

It becomes evident, during our brief encounters, that we are not going to make the Lower Chain Lake this afternoon. Nope, we will be content to stop at the first really good campsite and be satisfied with the day's progress. Mount Emmons is not climbed in a day.

When we finally reach Krebs Creek together, we are happy to reach a place where many others have halted. A fine-flowing stream, a musty meadow, a fire ring or six, good logs for sitting, a rock table, flat spots for a bivouac: all the good dividends of a happy reason to halt. A tall beetling ridge just south shuts off that part of the world: steep, imposing and boulder strewn. We are in the saucy highlands now. Eventually we will be much higher than these rocks and look down upon them. This is enough for today. There is rest, giblets, and valley tan for reward.

It is not until midmorning the next day that we see Mt. Emmons from the Lower Chain Lake. When we see it, we note two things simultaneously: it is clear which one of the rocky protuberances is Mt. Emmons, and it is still a long way to the summit. So disturbing is the view, in fact, that I am seized with a strong need to evacuate my bowels. It's a heckuva view, really. Tee and Sean are already fishing.

Lower Chain Lake is backed up by an earthen and rock dam, several dozen feet high, built, we speculate, during the CCC days. On the western shore of the lake, we can see a cart path, practically a road, still left over from those times. In fact, from Krebs we had followed a surprisingly wide trail—the width of two mules and a cart, anyway. All around the dam we have seen the construction material of those great, cooperative, socialist days. Big steel flumes, the remnants of an ancient wagon, old metal drums, the obligatory bedstead or two, a couple of woodstoves, more flumes—all this stuff was hauled way up here by mules pulling carts.

This type of material culture can still be found throughout the mining areas of the west. Whenever there was color in the hills—silver, lead, black or gold—a way was found to get to the stuff no matter where. In our rambles we have found cabins on ridge tops, mountain tops, noted cableways and trams, skirted many slag heaps and holes.

Western miners and their backers were industrious cusses. Certainly there were men and muleteers who would have known every bend and dip in that trail in the old days, every chicane and sand trap.

Then came the Civilian Conservation Corps and irrigation projects such as this at Lower Chain Lake. Here they were mining water, finding a way to carry it over from May and June until August and September. Looking for ways to support agriculture and grow the American economy.

We will discover and follow an old roadway

from the Lower to the Upper Chain Lakes. All in all, this place, for a few months in the 1930s, would have been a very good place to spend some time, ten times higher than the Chrysler Building and sweeter smelling.

The Lower Chain Lake is blue-green and slightly milky with the spring flow, but looks more on the sterile side than trout-teeming. All around the lake, except for this beach at the dam, is nothing but boulders. There are no friendly meadows to support afternoon hatches of mayflies and midges. It's austere and rugged, nothing like we had previously pictured. It's already hot. We eat lunch in the shade and set off for the end of the basin.

Hammered from the heat, though, and worn out from yesterday's labor, we reach the Upper Chain Lake and can't see any good reason to go beyond the sand-strewn inlet delta. Yes, we had hoped to hump to the Fourth Chain Lake, several hundred feet higher, up there, but we have to ask ourselves why?

"Why?"

"Why?"

"Why?"

With no good answer, we content ourselves with looking for a place to sleep. We find an old campsite, a mondo campsite, the Platonic form of killer campsite: a towering and well-maintained fire ring, great logs for sitting, a commodious flat rock for table and kitchen, and the ample shade of many an ancient fir. Clearly this campsite has been used for millennia, and well used, but fresh as tomorrow in early June. This is the right place; we will halt here.

Content, tuckered, we indulge some hours of restful hooky, angling our way to angling when the sun sinks lower on the horizon, when we may encounter brightly tugging cutthroats and brookies, who can say?

Tug they do.

Looking at maps and speculating for months, I had prognosticated with much vigor that an easy way would lead from the ridge above Roberts Pass to the top of Emmons. This ridge would be easy going, gravelly and soft, smooth sailing, a cakewalk with prizes. It would be no harder than smiling at a baby or clamping down the heels for a downhill run. The contour lines were widely spaced, clearly the ridge would not be steep. I staked my reputation, such as it was, on it, to encourage Tee and Sean to want to do it.

So easy it would be, said I to Tee and Sean, and anyone else who would listen (which, to be honest, was no one) that you could push a wheelbarrow up it. Not that a person might want to undertake that task, but that it surely could be done. And let's be clear, any wheelbarrow, from the skinny-wheeled garden variety that your grandma had, to a robust four-wheeler used in the trades—you could just up and push it along that ridge. If you happened to have one...a wheelbarrow. A big NO on the problem side.

How would this be possible? In addition to the wide spacing of the contour lines, experience has taught me that there are miles and miles of Uinta ridges that are endowed with gravel and schist or strewn with small talus. Okay, actually there are not, for there are many, many more miles that are home to the Death Platters, wiggly, wobbly, pit-pocketed big-thin stones, but that is no matter. True, the Death Platters take much concentration to cross, as they are prone to wobble, but which, all in all, provided they are not smeared with snow, or greased with ice, can provide relatively good going. Nor did I predict the Blocky Shifters, otherwise common. No, this ridge, Wheelbarrow Ridge, was low angle, not very steep, and it was sure to be easy and smooth and gravelly.

Rather I prophesized that Wheelbarrow Ridge would be a stroll on the alpine Champs Elysees, an easy turn down Via Tornabuoni.

In the early morning of June 13, 2007, there is a narrow cornice on the south edge of Wheelbarrow Ridge, made of Styrofoam snow. It makes for excellent footing between 7:53 and 9:38 am. This we do ascend: we take it because it's faster. Styrofoam snow, subject to repeated freeze and thaw, is nearly squeaky when frozen but highly unreliable as the day wears on. This cornice is about twenty feet wide, though often less, and it overhangs the death-dealing south face by four, five, six, seven, eight feet. Experienced mountaineers, we stay away from that edge, but the two dogs, Maggie and Boomer, repeatedly tramp left, right on the overhang. We call to them, often. We warn them. As dogs, they ignore us.

Sean, Tee and I stay on the very right-side edge of the slim cornice, afraid that one crack will send us down. I find myself still nervous when the snow pinches in to seven-or-eight feet in width, more cornice than not. Then I wander northerly onto the rocks, where progress ceases. The rocks make for slow going. We stick to the snow.

By the time we reach the steeper east face, a set of snowfields and red rocky shoals, the snow has already begun to soften. Up we go, double time.

By Hermes, it is cold on top! This is one of the chilliest summits I've ever embraced. An icebox norther at eighteen-and-a-half knots robs the pilgrim of any heat. Seriously. It's colder than winter up here. I put on every stitch I brought.

I unfurl stuff like magician from the daypack and don pants, overpants; fleece vest, light jacket; 'nother light jacket; cap, 'nother cap; gloves, overmitts. Bitterly cold, on this sunny June day.

On one side, this pleases me. There have been many peaks I have trod where most of the ridiculous overclothing remained in the rucksack. Not here.

Tee and Sean want to go off and bag a lower poorly-named peak to the west, a thirteen-thousander.

Actually, I'm good. Had enough for one day, thank you, my friends. Emmons means a whole lot.

"You go over there for table scraps, Chaps." I bid them good riddance and tell them I'll wait for them down below, somewhere where it is not so bloody cold.

How odd to be here on a cloudless and love-touched June day, but oh-so chilly at 13,440 feet. I snap a few and skedaddle. Glad to have gaiters, I plod down the snowfields to the upper saddle. The snow is getting right sloppy.

What a difference a thousand feet and orientation make. At the base of the face, in luxuriant thick sedges and grasses of a demi-heath, I face east, pull my boots off, make a pile of clothes and lay down, stick the anorak over my head, and prepare to nap awaiting Sean and Tee. Hell with them.

A person might suspect that the worst, most totally awful and immediately threatening conditions in high mountains are found in steep and shadowed places. There is certainly some truth to this, but most sensible people know to avoid steep and shadowed places.

It is actually easiest to get lost in tree-filled, gently-rolling, non-descript terrain. In a canyon, at least you know where the bottom is — where the stream is — and what that means. There's up and there's down. In a land of rolling ups and downs, however, everything can begin to look the same, with just enough trees and not enough distant landmarks. Or if the landmarks are simply ridges as they are in the Uintas, it doesn't take long to get disoriented.

Frequently in the Uintas some hapless soul wanders off, gets confused, gets lost, gets scared, gets injured, and gets snuffed when the first storm with the white wind rolls in.

Actually some of the worst places are level or gently sloping. These are very deceptive too: You think it will be good, but it can turn bad quickly. And it's flat. Flat! The surprise may not be pleasant.

For example, I would have to say that for blister-building, morale-destroying, ankle-tweaking agony, few places can equal a dry Wheelbarrow Ridge. Tee and Sean rejoin me, ready to finish the downward task.

The styrofoam snow of early morning is

too mushy to cross. How mushy? Mushy to the bottom, impossible to negotiate. We must take to the rocks. The dry rocks feature some of the most tedious footing possible, and there's no way to get around it. Sharp, up-ended stones cover it entirely, portside to starboard. Each step is a twist on point, each stride a turn. We have to balance on sharp grainy arrowheads of rock, point to point, never big enough for security or comfort. They don't wiggle or slip, they're solid—solid like pins in a big red pincushion. It's like walking across the crystals of a geode, like dancing across rocks to cross a stream but without the stream.

> We split up to see if we can find a better way.
> "How is it?"
> "Bad."
> "Worse."
> "The worst."
> "Will it get better?"
> "It has to."
> Actually, it doesn't have to.
> Usually the way down is much easier than the way up. This is not the case on Wheelbarrow Ridge.
> In my den, in my dreams, with maps spread on Sean McHelen's table as we fondled the contour lines, it looked like twenty minutes of dog-trotting would get us up or down the ridge. The imaginary gravelly/schisty slopes would be easy.
> The actual descent is going to take five or seven times that much. It will take hours.
> The gaps between the pointy rocks reach out for the legs of the mountaineer, hoping to award a compound fracture medallion on the tib-fib of the trespasser, with white bone bursting out through the pale fleshy bits, and the arterial spurting, or at least

the regular vessels oozing crimson onto the sharp red rocks as shock sets in.

It isn't steep. It isn't cold. In fact, it's pretty darned hot. Each step is a visit to the dentist, the preparation for some endoscopy work, a letter from the IRS, a note informing you of an increased retainer from your lawyer. It seems that this might become Wheelchair Ridge. Or Helicopter Rescue Ridge. Call for one now! Wheelbarrow — yes, carry me out in one. Please.

As we say in the trade, we'd gladly trade ten miles of Death Platters for this horrendous stretch. We'd rather climb up some greasy, schisty, rain-soaked, slippery-slope gully than the dog-breath delight that is the East Ridge of Mt. Emmons.

By the time we reach the typical red-and-purple garbage that leads from the ridge down to Robert's Pass, it seems like a path strewn with primrose compared to the pincushion back there.

I am not a person who likes to give route advice or guidance, but a note to all future visitors: Unless it's entirely covered with snow, for your own sanity and safety, stay away from the Wheelbarrow Ridge of Mt. Emmons, Brothers and Sisters, AWAY!

At the pass I observe that the crossing has ripped open holes in my Italian leather hiking boots, gill slits, separating the toe rand from the rest of the upper, greatly improving the footwear's ventilation. The boots are no longer waterproof but very breathable. I say bad things about the Italian boot brand and worse things about Wheelbarrow Ridge.

The gill slits, however, do look remarkably like the ones on my Gallardo Spyder.

I really wish I had that remarkable machine with me now, right here to warm up and rev a bit. Gallardo, *tesoro mio*. We could drive around the delta, do some donuts in the sand.

Feeding trout are roiling the surface of the Upper Chain Lake as we pass it, hobbling. It hurts. We say we'll hike back up after a lovely little rest but know we won't. We're too tired back at camp to do anything except the bare essentials. The shade from ancient fir helps assuage the haircuts in the middle of our somas.

We limp and shuffle down to Krebs for an easy day on the next one, glad to leave the Chains behind. Krebs is good. Krebs is a snake-twist stream, avalanche lilies, winter-matted grasses, pale fire, and the promise of six/eight miles on the morrow. Hell was back there. Hell was Wheelbarrow Ridge. Hell was guessing and being wrong. Hell was a bristling pincushion of sharp rough rocks. Hell, look what happened to my Italian leather boots.

As we drive toward town, I imagine a reward:

At Café Emmons in Roosevelt we begin with a delicate brook trout bisque, paired with an ale sampler, followed by an antipasto of heirloom sun-dried tomatoes, Throube olives, hand-squeezed artichokes, two kinds of elk salami and one of pronghorn. *Coppia ferrarese*, of course. This we pair with a Napa pinot noir. Subsequent to this, some Bear Lake raspberry sorbet and a dollop of Frascati.

Our first plate is *gnocchi a la ragazzina*, done

in a fennel and shitake sauce, washed down with a stout Bardolino. The second plate is a smoked local splake filet and a ceviche of cutthroat roe touched with sage, paired with chilled Blanc de Blanc. The third features elk medallions finished with a rambunctious port glaze and shaved black truffles. Cote du Rhone, of course. This last course is extra tasty. We beg for seconds. *"Oui, Messieurs,"* says the *garçon*. We receive three more delicious portions!

The two salads which follow, the first a simple *insalata mista* with juniper-berry vinagrette, the second the old-standby pear and gorgonzola, sprinkled with Neola pine nuts, help us regain our edge. But the cheese and fruit array, and bottles of Moscato d'Asti, tawny port and Washington State Riesling pretty much do us in. We draw the line at the digestifs.

The bill comes to $1,934.89, and it is graciously picked up and shared by Tee and Sean. We toss many fifties on the table gratuitously.

"Hey, it sure was great not just walking with you guys, but eating together was swell," I say. "Thanks for the meal. That was truly grand."

"Way grand," says Sean.

"Grand."

The Roosevelt Burger King is in an old filling station. It's quite fitting, actually.

"Never again," says Tee, outside, looking away. "Emmons, Shmemmons."

"My swellings are swollen," I say. "Ouch."

"Wheelchair or walker," adds Sean, touching his shoulder. "Help me, somebody."

Scrambling High Unita Peaks

"You sure you're okay to drive, McHelen?"
"Drive?"
"Who's driving?"
"Don't drive with that crown on, Tee."
"Sean's driving. I'm going to sleep."
"Adios, amigos."

Boreal Toads

In May, well before the snow is gone, by a pond, ringed with snowdrifts, or a very wet wetland still icy in the mornings, or a lake, the shores of which are yet drifted on, you will hear the inane croakings of some creature. This is in the daytime, the morning or afternoon. It's some ribbity creature, grooving on an old vibration. You cannot miss them, but you can mistake them.

The croaks come in waves of call and response, with silence in between. The ribbits are loud and you can hear them across the meadow, and then they stop, and then it all starts up again. You wonder what beast makes such a harmonious racket. It sure sounds like an amphibian, a frog or toad, but that's impossible because there is still much snow, and amphibians, being cold blooded, are not drawn to snow, to say nothing of the elevation (over nine thousand feet). "No way," you say. "That ain't no reptile much less an amphibian."

A bit of research reveals its handle: the boreal toad. Wow! Really? Well it's cold blooded, check it and see. Choirs of strong singers in the early spring. Ribbiters with song sounds that roll like waves. All hail toads of the north!

Boreal toads perform just one of the many critter songs.

This time of year, if you are at the right place at the right time, by a pond or lake with some snow still surrounding it, you will hear the rhythmic ribbiting of the boreal toad, as we've observed. Croak-a-licous!

Add to this it is not unusual to note the honk of Canada geese passing over in vees, trying to get back together again or thronged upon yonder shore. What can be said of geese can also apply to ducks, and more: a lot of them are willing to talk-that-trash at once. To this is added the possibility of the throat-song of sandhill cranes gliding in wide circles above, beyond, and back on the ground, for it's love time for cranes.

No day is complete without the playful wails of coyotes, heard in the morning across the way, in the afternoon upon a breeze, or at dusk warming up a show in the Ryman.

You've got your snipes, yes, snipes, and don't put it past an owl pair to occasionally join in the call and response in yonder spruce and fir forest. Cacophony it is. Springtime in the Rockies.

And rarely, a loon.

Roseate

All these benefits, that mountaineering gives us, are produced to a great extent by two psychological processes which are typical of mountaineering:

Physical elevation is always associated with a symbolic elevation. The young man who, looking down to the valley, sees himself so much higher than the others, feels for a moment stronger, stronger than the others down there and stronger than he was before leaving the valley.

The collective facing of risk — in the mountains or on his return to the valley the mountaineer is rarely alone — fosters a social recognition which reinforces the feeling of strength and self-confidence (all mountaineers to an extent seek this social recognition: did any of us, on his return from an ascent in the mountains, refrain from telling the tale ?).

— Bernard Amy, 2013

Scrambling High Unita Peaks

I know for a fact that Mount Lovenia was named by a government surveyor for his fiancée, later wife, Lovenia, and that they were lucky to have been happy in life, their happiest times perhaps spent in a rough cabin on Chalk Creek way back when, because their daughter, Suzanne, wrote me a letter about it after she read "The Longest Day" in a magazine. Surely this bit of backstory highlights the idealism in the beauties in the world of love and nomenclature. So-named, Lovenia will outlast all of us, a record of that love.

Having tried on two separate occasions to find myself atop lofty Mount Lovenia, and failed, and ended up in the dumps because of it, I realize that life is too short and the effort too great to support another unsuccessful try. Not that the walking in the East Fork isn't fine, the scenery grand and the wildlife abundant, but this time I will not fail. Period. No matter the weather or the noises in my head. If it takes three tries, then the way is three times longer, the reward three times as great. Three is less than four. There will be no four.

Naturally I have to find the right partner. I have already made it most of the way with Larry Darkness and Tee Trundler, and watched, petting my bunions while they added the big L to their lists. I would not ask them to go again, and if I did, I'm sure they would refuse.

Sean McHelen is the obvious choice, being

credulous, youthful and eager to encrust this red-faceted jewel on his tiara.

The attempt starts months before we meet at the trailhead. Invariably when I visit him in Salt Lake City, at some point the maps will be whipped out and the talk will grow puffy, steep and ridiculous. Routes will be prognosticated with much putrid palaver. As we've seen, maps will be spread out in the living room with Larissa nearby, and just as invariably, she will grow sleepy as we drone on about this way and that, what to leave in, what to leave out, and she will begin sawing logs after a few minutes of our seminar, putting our quest into perspective.

Still, Sean and I stand committed. Larissa will stay behind, pregnant in the event, with far more important business to take care of.

There is a slim window of opportunity of optimum times for a jaunt to the East Fork. The flanks of the Uintas can be visited in all seasons, and have been, and should be. And actually the posse have climbed worthy peaks from May to October, and January, and skied them from December to May (thanks for asking), but the prime time is only six or seven weeks long: from the last week in July to the second week in September. Earlier than that are ice-girt mornings, then bugs and flowing bogs, sodden hummocks, and dangerous stream crossings; later is cold and the chance for snow, followed by the actual fact of snow and ice and steady white winds.

Uinta peaks, so richly endowed with talus, cannot be ascended after the first or second snow — when the days are still tolerably long, since snowed-up, ice-topped talus presents merely a thousand ways to break a leg or badly scrape one's caboose. Waiting until there is enough cover only adds to the difficulties. August it will be.

Determined, I drive to the East Fork trailhead with my focus steadfast, stopping only to pick up some firewood in a roadside clearing. It's early enough to take a late day stroll. The campground is empty in the middle of the week. Just beyond the north edge of the parking lot, I spy two moose, a mama and a calf. They walk toward me, haven't smelled me, and I have to cower behind a slim lodgepole, short on cover, as they pass less than fifty feet away. It is a good omen and keeps the string of moose sightings intact (at least one per trip for several years.)

Satisfied with the omen, I go back to the truck, start a fire and wait for Sean. He arrives on schedule, and we enjoy a productive supper with the governor on.

I have pared my gear back to a nearly-ignorable thirty-six pounds, fully watered. This tilts the odds in my favor, as my general conditioning leaves something to be desired. In-shape Sean, on the other hand, always likes to bring the kitchen sink in his pack, though this time it's a hammered-brass wet bar sink with a swan-necked faucet and copper-infused sprayer. His pack can't weigh much more than fifty pounds, evening it up somewhat.

Our plan is simple: walk as far back into the East Fork as we can, certainly to the Terrace, and then set up camp, rest on our camp mats, and hope for good weather for the summit.

RED STONE HEART

Even though I've walked the entirety of this canyon at least two times through Many Moose Meadows, the forests and Terrace, none of it seems familiar, beyond the vague familiarity of all Uinta Mountain patterns. As we walk, I try to reconstruct those past trips but soon give up. Enough years have passed between that the separateness is indistinguishable. I've almost never walked the same trail twice, certainly never passed this way before.

After a third rest stop we struggle with the one big hill below the Terrace, lose the trail, curse the spruce and embrace the fir before we gain the upper land. It's one o'clock in the Intermountain West and unbelievably hot. Stinking hot, really, another reason we're glad we left early. We have to sit in the shade to even stand it. Hot at eleven thousand feet? Over eighty degrees? This must be why all the trees are dying back. When we look at them closely we see marks of stress on all the limbs and needles. It's happening....

Lovenia stands at the end of the valley. We're closer now and can see her not-very-lovely north face features: she's a rotten old dame these days, tumbled down and busted up. She, who is so impressive, imposing from afar, just doesn't draw looks of love but rather awe up close.

We tip our hats to the dozen unnamed summits that stand between the East Fork and the Little East one, pink and red ridges and talus chutes, steep and sunburning in the heat haze, an agglomeration of savage business. Across the valley to the west rise Wasatch, Tokeanother and Tokewanna, a massively undulating ridgeline of grays and buffs and greens. The place where we had hoped to camp (from map gazing and pre-pin-pointing) is waterless this year, so we push on along the Terrace.

We spend an hour finding the perfect spot. A grainy flat rock of purple-red, eighty square feet in extent, will provide an excellent camp table, complete with shelves and a complimentary rock stash for a matching fire ring. A rivulet gurgles no more than one hundred paces away. A few spruce surround for shade and friendship. What seals the spot is the herd of mascot elk that can be seen grazing across the valley right at the base of a peak, not close, but clearly visible. I spot them first, two dozen or so. Right across the valley. Those aren't horses, Sean, they're elk, Wapiti, note the chocolate necks and white rumps, up as high as we are and surely sweltering. The elk!

We set up our sleeping places. I've brought only a tarp, Sean his lightest tent, repaired with duct tape where a Wind River bear recently hugged it, just trying to say howdy-do. Mr. Beam appears, so too does Sean's Mp3 player with speakers. We kick way back, look at Lovenia, rest our wearies and ready our minds for the morrow.

Granted an Mp3 player with speakers is hardly zero-impact, but we haven't seen anyone all day, and the elk are too far way to matter—or to care—so we rock out and roll along. Team America, Spamalot, John Prine, the Pixies. It passes the time (and he carried it).

It would be wrong to say that the north face of Lovenia is pleasant to look at. The climbing possibilities are downright ugly as well. Last time I was here Tee went right up it, but it was snow-covered, and The Trundler Direct would be idiotic to try in late summer. Nothing but loose blocks and rotten cliffs. The face is split by a horizontally-tending large red line that runs from high west to lower east. Some of the cliffs are stained black with what looks like coal. Massive talus gullies spill down from the batwing ridges. The lower guardian cliffs look in bad repair.

I can plainly see the Dumbest Traverse and wonder aloud how Larry and I could have been so foolish, so wrong, such dumb asses back in 1992. I look at Sean and no longer wonder. With age comes wisdom. I'm living proof of that. Young Kevin is Well-Into-Middle-Age Kevin now, a repository of wisdom, a suppository of sage.

We study the western flanks and ridges to see if there's a decent way up. Between the peak and shoulder debouches a steep and direct gully that might provide a good way down and a terrible way up. Farther west, we spy a shorter gully that looks to be the best of our ascent options. It leads up to a little col between the north face and the East Fork Pass. We take a stroll at sunset to get a better look at it, and feel hopeful that it's the best way.

Dawn finds us leaving camp and walking up the basin in the early light. Long shadows stretch and grasses whisper in the breeze. How fine and bracing it is to be way up here, just now. We pass pothole lakes and balustrades of ruddy quartzite and revel in expansive views. The hag north-east face is darkly gloomy.

As we approach the gully, it looks steeper than it did last evening. We hope we made the right choice. It turns out to be a talus palace in the bottom, slimy in the middle, and rich with schist toward the top. Up we go until the schist slaps us silly.

What other mountain ground is quite as hard to ascend as good old Uinta schist? Uneven layers of down-sloping, friable, greasy blue-black schist, larded with rockfall from above and dolloped with baby-turd yellow lines of mudstone. We fight our way up. For every step upward, we slide back down half the distance. We are forced to all fours, bear crawling before the mountain goddess.

Hot and sweaty in the gully, once we crest out of it, a cold southwest breeze snatches us. The south face looks suddenly steep and sustained. We sit down out of the wind, catch our breath, and try not to look at it. To avoid the south face (endless boulders on open slopes) we'll have to scramble up the gendarme ridge. We're hoping the gendarmes are easy to disarm, or that they can be bribed into submission by our *élan,* or simply overpowered by our *joie de vivre.*

We see the distant peaks of the Wasatch: Mt. Timpagnosis and Hidden Peak among them. We spy two moose by a pothole lake down below in Lambert Meadow. It is 9:00 a.m. and we are well up Lovenia.

The ridge, though cliffy, gives way easily. A remnant goat path leads up and through the clifflet rubble. At the mouth of the escape gully, the one we had looked at yesterday as a possible descent route, we decide that it'll be a goer for the way down. I dump my pack, grab a camera and a snack, scramble up the white-tan summit boulders, and by 10:30 we are on top of Lovenia.

I try to reach my mother by cellphone but have no luck. She suffers from Alzheimer's and lives in a special facility, but for some reason I want to talk to her and tell her what it's like on top of this mountain. I've not been able to reach her, though, for some years.

I leave a message at my home in Green River. We leave a restrained message at Tee's. Sean rings Larissa, fills her in...blah blah blah.

It's almost hot on the summit. There is no wind. It's possible to see the other highest Uinta peaks, or at least most of them, and name them from the cloudless top.

I hold up eight fingers and one thumb to show Sean. Nine, comrade. The Notorious Nine. I count in Italian for Emilio Comici and Walter Bonatti and Reinhold. *Uno, due, tre...*

Finally, all nine peaks are mine, not mine, but done, finished, climbed, d-o-n-e. I mention to Sean that it feels good. He congratulates me and says he feels good, too. His eight is nearly my nine. He says he probably doesn't feel quite as good as I do, but that he feels plenty good. Oh, yeah.

After a short reflection, I tell him that I feel REALLY GOOD. That's a lot of steps over a lot of years, Brother. And I tell him I could not possibly feel any better.

I remember the nine. Sean doesn't ask but I name them: Kings, Wasatch, (Kings again), South Kings, Tokewanna, Gilbert, Wilson, Powell, Emmons, Lovenia. In that order. The best saved for last? Looo-o-o-o-oove-e-e-e-enia! Who cares? I say the names again. All above thirteen thousand, the Notorious Nine, the highest mounds of rock in the state. They form a list of pretty great days. Some good summits, some dark summits. All nine, all mine, in a line, very fine.

And yet it is all somewhat unsettling. We

are not meant to live up this high, nor spend more time than necessary, really. Still, we have plenty of time today.

I study the Wasatch-to-Tokewanna ridge and remember Mark and Tee and me. Wasatch rises gray-green, ugly and scary. So much just jutting and sky catching. Tokewanna simply looms, a gigantic wreck, with Tokeanother between them. So much is back then and over there.

So much.

And all the rivers that start here, and the many ways they make their ways, and all the canyons, that make a way, having been made to make a way by water.

And all the sky-catching lakes. And all the streams in the highest meadows that flow over polished rocks. Brown-bottomed, dark-flowing streams.The spring stream surge. Water flowing down through blocky canyons ringed with arrowy trees.

The lingering snowdrifts and avalanche lilies. The forests of lodgepole pine, and the places beneath pines where we sleep. To sleep and awaken to birdsong. Black-capped chickadees and pine siskins. Towhees. Heart attack grouse in the forest. Ravens, owls, hawks, osprey and eagles in snags by the rivers.

The songs of coyotes. The laughter of coyotes. The joshing of coyotes.

And all the rocky memories of glaciers. Lime-green lichens on purple-red rocks. Orange lichens on purple-and-buff striped ridgetop rocks and boulders. Rocks polished by the glaciers.

Rocks moved by the glaciers. Rocks left alone by the glaciers. Polished rocks. Buried rocks. Very old rocks. No new rocks, only new parts of old rocks.

Snow-white ermines leaving small tracks on snow. Snowshoe hares blending in with the snow except for eyes and nose. Spiders on snow. Red fungus on snow. Snow on snow and more snow. Skiing on snow. Sliding on snow. Avalanches of snow, snapping trees and settling on hillsides going uphill the other way: One of the ways that water flows uphill. Amphitheaterical: the big cirques at the upper ends of valleys, places for winds to howl, snows to mingle.

In the centuries of Lake Bonneville, the snowstorms were outrageous. Consider a very large lake seven hundred miles from the Pacific. Consider a freshwater lake as large as Superior. Consider mountains two-and-a-half-miles high. Consider a hundred feet of snow a season. Consider 206 snow-storm days per year. Consider this for centuries.

Consider the avalanches that were caused by that snow. Consider the way avalanches move, compact and concentrate snow. Deep snow turning to ice, turning upon itself, making glaciers.

Is it any wonder the glaciers stretched forty miles? Or that it took a long time for them to melt. Or that today the trees in the upper basin are dying back, showing stressed red needles at the base of every branch? Or that these spruce and fir are niche organisms, and all living things are niche organisms. Or that many and much of the lodgepole has already died back because of pine beetles, because of raised temperatures, because of warmer winters, because of climatic changes, because of burning carbon?

Scrambling High Unita Peaks

Are the elk niche organisms? They move. They are managed and valued. They are hunted and eaten. Few hunt them way back here. No place is finer than the places elk spend their august days. They have learned through generations where the best places are. Such places are good and good in elk memory.

Almost no one cares about these trees.

And what about the pika? They live in the boulder fields, year-round. They gather hay and bleat. We invade their living rooms and they bleat back at us. As the change approaches them, will they move? Can they move, these pikas? Or will their bleats just fade away?

We make our way down the steep escape gully. I am glad I have poles. I use them for balance in the ankle-teasing talus. The fall line leads down into steep and curvy gullies. We veer east and right to avoid the gullies, kick steps for purchase, and keep to the face. Sean falls because he does not use poles. He does not use poles because he fancies he is young and does not need to use poles. Poles are good. Someday he will use poles to keep his sorry ass from the rocky ground. As it is, he falls now and then because the terrain is steep and slippery. I am glad I have poles. I love my poles.

The slope is long and colorful. When you learn to use gravity, kick places for your feet, you lean into the downward but not too far. The downward is your friend, but not a good friend. Someone to use, not someone to love. You must edge when it is steep. You must be wary. The fall-line sucks you into bad places, a little ball-bearing-loose gravel over hard rock that sends you down, quickly down.

We are sweating by the time we reach the bottom of the slope. Grass starts and thistles begin. A few more hundred yards to go. We halt where the busted-up meets the grass, and we say hey, now.

Yet we need shade. We find our way back to camp. We sit in shade and take care of business.

Larissa is going to have a baby.

Sean is going to be a daddy.

I try to tell Sean what it means to be a daddy. It is a very good thing. It gives people like us a chance to learn about love.

It is way better than not being a daddy. It is different.

I love my Christopher so much it makes me shed happy tears talking about it. And the girls, too.

Across the valley the elk mill. The young ones run. Their coats shine golden-white and brown against the golden meadows, the darker trees, the sweep of pink rock slopes.

We sit in the shade, cook, swill and feel pretty good about it. I brought freeze dried food and we eat it. We listen to silly music. We listen to silence.

My bed is under a tarp arranged between two trees. I cut the back of my hand this morning on one of the branches when not quite awake. It bled but didn't hurt: a two-inch-long superficial scratch that bled. The cut is good: I drew blood but not in battle. The scar will remain in prominence for two full years. Then it will no longer be there prominently. Where does it go?

The afternoon stretches. We are tired and do not want to move. We look at Lovenia's North Face and see the red. We are glad that we did not embrace that red. The rocks are red. The blood from my hand is red. The bourbon is amber-red. The needles on the spruce are red. The large flat grainy rock that is our table is red. The rocks that will ring our fire are red.

When we build the fire it will be orange and red.

The next day we will get lost between the Terrace and the river. Quite badly lost, but we know which way is down. We eventually find the trail.

As we walk the whole of the East Fork clouds threaten with big talk and dust devils and spitting rain. We don't dare stop for lunch, not wanting to get soaked.

We talk about the food we have at the car. We think about the food that we talk about having at the car. We walk without stopping. We stop the talk.

Why is it that I'm always in the East Fork, walking without stopping?

Only a few droplets fall. We reach the cars. We heat and eat the food we talked about. Our cars are trucks. We eat beans and potatoes and salsa and chips and cheese and cerveza. The taste is a very good taste.

We drive down to the reservoir and down to the-you've-got-to-be-joking boat ramp. I jump into the water. It's breathtaking. It is cold but I like cold water. It feels very good to swim in the cold water, the snow-fed water, the snowfield water.

From the water's edge we can almost see Lovenia.

Disintegration

November, 2007.

I have come here as No-Longer-Young-Kevin because I haven't for thirty years. In season there are good reasons not to come to Holiday Meadow, as it is a-throttle with dispersed recreationalists of all descriptions, owing to its ease of access and attractive location.

Also because to come here means confronting ghosts. Some years in November this place is already snowed in. This is not some years. True, there are a few snowdrifts, but the campground is empty. The nymphs are departed.

Sean McHelen and I meet up at Bear River to assay the late season situation and pick the spot. We have brought firewood and will gather still more.

Scrambling High Unita Peaks

Tee should be here. But Tee has become Amblin' Teemore Shufflesworth. Say it again. Amblin' Teemore Shufflesworth. It's as bad as it sounds. There's trouble with Teemore.

We have been trying to get him to come out and play, but Teemore is having psychic difficulties just now. A combination of pressure at work, middle age funk, too much time out to lunch, and obviously some chemical imbalances caused him to have a full-on breakdown a couple of months ago, complete with a suicide attempt. Teemore needed some help, got some help, is intent on getting better.

To be frank, I'm worried. He visited me in Green River changed from the Tee of old. Part of my agenda is to get Sean to watch out for Teemore. He lives in the same town—Salt Lake City—and they go to Jazz games and ski together. Maybe he'll get better. Maybe this had to happen. Maybe he hasn't hit bottom yet. Maybe he'll never be the same. (Of course, he'll never be the same. None of us is.)

Clarence King had a breakdown, lived a secret life and died alone in Tucson, Arizona.

Middle-Aged Kevin is not the Young Kevin he was at this campground with Mark Alpenglow all those years ago. Or yet he is, surely. That time, having been chased down the blizzardy slopes and ridges of Lamotte Peak by Zeus the Thunderer, we were so amped and happy to have made it back alive, that we spent many hours here delightedly bellowing, swilling and dancing, washed clean by the experience. Here I understood the pull of Dionysus, the affirmation that comes from life-intoxication and abandon. Although I have often sought to revive that feeling, it can never be reclaimed. It drifts off like campfire smoke, leaving scarred rocks behind.

To be here this afternoon where the Stillwater runs deep is to be surrounded by these high peaks of memories. In the 1980s, the ancient past, I climbed each snow-capped peak I can see: Lamotte, Ostler, Spread Eagle, Agassiz, Hayden, A-1, Kletting. I remember the routes and some details of the day. So what? Who cares?

I think about my companions and my younger brother, Gary, with whom I ascended Agassiz in 1984. We took a backpacking trip with our parents. Our father, already suffering from Parkinson's disease, our mother quite spry and steadily eager. It was a great thing to do—to take one's fifty-nine year old parents into the wilderness. Gary and I took our time and carried most of the stuff. We set up camp in a scenic meadow and enjoyed a few days in the wild.

One day we scrambled up the gray, loose East Face of Agassiz. Gary hasn't climbed mountains since, but he does play bass and keys in classic rock tribute bands in So-Cal. Classic rock, that Agassiz.

My father is gone now. The Parkinson's was somewhat treated by drugs, but there were times when it was a grim, sad battle. My mother suffers from Alzheimer's. A cruel disease, as we all know, that eats away at the victim's memory. She still recognizes me, knows my name, knows my son's name, but her world is growing ever-smaller. I'll learn that someday she will at least know I'm someone she's supposed to know even if she can't quite place me.

Scrambling High Unita Peaks

Memoirists don't want to get Alzheimer's. I don't want my mother to have it, but I recognize no choice in the matter. Cancer, Parkinson's and/or Alzheimer's—aye, gather ye rosebuds while ye may.

Holiday Meadow with its postcard view every time you turn around, is about gathering rosebuds, surely. Memories of great days, things that mattered, people to do it with. No one can say I didn't have my share of time in the mountains.

Coyotes have carved dens into an old sandy morainal bank on the south end of the campground. I need some time to sift, so while Sean goes off to gather more wood, I look at the triumvirate panorama. Ostler, No Name, Spread Eagle.

Hell, it's only the big Five-O I'm looking at, but I don't think I'll be doing too much peak bagging in the future. And Sean is nine years younger, which matters at the end of one's glorious career. We can try something different, perhaps.

Sure, Sean's got time, but he will probably never have this perfect horseshoe of peaks on his stringer. But even for Peter Pans like us, when you start to look at forty, (or fifty) your priorities change. They should. His life is about to change in ways he can't imagine. Larissa and Sean are about to have a baby, a mortal anchor to keep you closer to home. Nobody gets to be a better person by peddling a bicycle...or slogging peaks. Just thicker laurels.

How about trying to be a better husband, Kevin, or a better father? Maybe a better friend? Hate to even say it, but a better professor? The way you've lived leaves plenty of room for improvement, nothing but room for improvement.

I guess I'll start on those the day after

tomorrow. Tonight, we have this firelight agenda and have to cover some items that have to do with Teemore.

It's not as though we haven't seen the signs. Teemore getting careless. Teemore getting obsessive about stupid, pointless things. I've watched him pack and repack and repack his backpack a dozen times. Teemore losing his application instrument in the dark. Teemore being ridiculous about driving: either way too fast or way too slow. Teemore taking too much time to break camp. Teemore being passive-aggressive. Teemore taking naps. The sick games Teemore and Lady Teemore play, a mountain of dishes in the sink and no fresh *leche* in the fridge.

He was always the one who was in control when the situation got dicey, could find a way down no matter what. Plus, Tee has always been damned fun, Teemore not so much. All the peaks we have slogged together don't seem to be helping right now.

This last stretch has not been much fun. Teemore, skinny and scared, and variable and vulnerable and scattered and nothing like he used to be.

Sure, he's depressed. Who isn't? There's no real reason not to be depressed just because existence is hopeless and has no meaning. Seriously? Why wouldn't a thinking person be down in the dumps from time to time? Depression, sure, I got my hand on that wheel pretty firmly. How do we deal with it? For Teemore it's going out to lunch, too much of the herbal supplement, too much time sampling the buffet. He's tried to quit it and ends up almost an invalid. Each time he starts up again, he starts up again more fully. Sometimes it's just ridiculous. In the parking lot, have a helping. Oh look at that nice tree, have another. Oh, a stream, *uno mas por favor*, and so on. Get so far out there it's not clear if it's possible to come back.

Self-medication—certainly I've got little room to talk much about that—but to get him off the addiction, they got him on some right strong stuff and that shit messes with your mind like the high test. It has side effects that are unpredictable. He takes naps for hours. He's lost the mania of the previous Tee Trundler, out in front, darkening Lovenia and Kings and Gilbert in a day.

Of course I want to make it better, even if I don't know exactly how to pull it off. I've known him for more than thirty years. He's been there for me in his own way, but I really don't know what to do. Or I'm too chicken to do it, just watching from shore as the ships go down.

When I climbed this horseshoe of peaks individually and together I did it solely for myself. No one helps anyone else climbing mountains. I'm not sure if you even help yourself, but you might. Along the way I found some people I really do care about, saw some fabulous things, felt a variety of emotions, some strongly, and did nothing to improve the world or humanity.

Jennifer says I won't get Alzheimer's because I'm so nasty, though she says it in a nice way. I hope she's right. Without these memories what would I have? When I drive over Highway 150, I cannot see a peak that I have not climbed, and that feels right.

So we have a fireside chat. Sean will keep an eye on him, try to get him to come out. We'll do what we can do. But for me it's a bit of cop out, trying to shift my responsibility to someone else.

Amblin' Teemore Shufflesworth....

We get him to come out skiing but he's still excessive. We take some trips to the mountains, but they're on different terms. He starts to act erratically. Back home he collects guitars and spends a lot of money on guitars. He thinks about guitars. He repairs guitars. The map room becomes his guitaritorium. The climbing wall, he demolishes.

It gets to be real hard to get him to come out, and when he does, it's a drag. We try to play guitar together but it's different. He's a competent player, and dedicated, but we're not together or in tune anymore.

When we get together in the mountains, we try to make it like old times, like the time Tee sang all of "Landslide," nearly as fine as Stevie herself, in the back seat of a car on the way to Astral Bounder's wedding. Or the time we did the entire *Born to Run* album in the parking lot at the Gate Buttress because it was raining too hard to climb. But we don't go in the same cars anymore, we don't sing, and there ain't no Clarence now.

When we move to Ogden, I'm hoping things will be different. They aren't.

It takes five years. There are high lonesome days. It seems like he's working on Ian Tyson's song: "If the good times are all gone, then I'm bound for moving on; I'll look for you if I'm ever back this way."

Skiing from time to time, too. Teemore skis on planks as wide as snowboards, and well, and often, and we hope that may rekindle the fires, but it's not enough.

At times, it's just not as fun as it used to be. He's become rather exasperating and unreliable. He takes a sabbatical from work, hoping to get his head together, because he can't pass the next-level security test. I don't see him too often, but we email regularly. He goes back to work half-time, and we try to be supportive. It's just a security test. I send him an email asking if there's anything I can do to help. He briefly responds with "No."

He said "No" because he'd already made his plan, which he executes a few days later.

In late March, 2012, he brings down the curtain with a shotgun blast to the chest spraying blood and tissue on the walls of all our lives.

I stand in front of a group in the Larkin Mortuary to read a story from Big Wonderful that stars Tee, ("The Longest Day") because Lady Teemore asked me to. And before I begin, I ask, "How many of you have been on top of a mountain with Teemore, excuse me, Tee Trundler?"

And pretty much everyone in that room raises his or her hand.

"Yeah," I say. "He was good that way. Tee Trundler...I've been on top of five dozen mountains with him. Five dozen, and yes, I did count."

I'm struck as I look out at the hundred people in that room — smart, educated, fit, outdoorsy — decent people, and some of their children, and I'm not sure anyone really understands or ever will. And that's what brings us together. The knowing and the not knowing. The mystery and the crimson stars.

And we miss him on the slopes, right then, for he was a very fine skier, free heel and clampdown, hands up or hands down. A telemarker who paralleled with desperate style and grace. We're left with tracks covered by the next storm.

Teemore's exit casts shadows. The first time Don Durancos and I sit down alone to talk about what happened to our best friend, we don't say much. We sit silently for a long time in the sunroom of the studio in Good Water and just let it sink in. Finally, we talk a little. It's okay not to say much, we agree, because we still have to carry it around for a time.

Choice is a slippery fish. For a long time I'm not sure if Teemore felt he had a choice, because things weren't getting better, and there was a certain inevitability that I could trace, thinking about all the conversations we'd had. It wasn't surprising, just sad.

The second time is nearly a year later, same location. Durancos and I spend some time talking about spending time with it. We agree that we can be sad about it anytime we want to, and no one could say that we'd neglected those feelings, but we are going to choose not to think about it, not to dwell on it, but to get past it. We never say that's what he would have wanted, because that's bullshit. He did what he wanted and we were left with the wreckage, and the choice to pick up the pieces and carry on.

Because in the end that's how you overcome it. You get angry, and you say you were an ass, and you say WTF, and then you decide to think about other things. That's what Don and I agree to, and it's important.

The silver lining, too, is that Durancos and I have grown closer. When there was the threesome, it was always two against one. It had to be because we both wanted Tee to be our favorite pardner. And as duos, Don and Tee, and Tee and me, we had separate memories and jolly good times. In those days sometimes I was jealous and hated Don J. Durancos.

But when it's just the two of us now, everything seems to change, and it seems to me that's exactly as it should be. The gray beard gang needs to have learned at least one thing from all those decades in the hills: That each day, each powder run, every peak and all the lakes and rivers are gifts. There's a number on each and every one — even when sometimes it seems those times could last forever. Knowing that we'd never take another trip with Tee Trundler, too, makes it easy to reminisce, but we also want to move forward.

My relationship with Sean McHelen, though, suffers. It's not hard to guess at the reason. It's the necessary fallout of the fireside chat at Holiday Meadow. We both blame each other, even knowing that, in the end, we probably did everything that we could do, except that we didn't. I put impossible demands on Sean because I couldn't deal with it, conveniently living far away, and having a fair bit on my plate. I think that, likewise, it was inevitable that he's felt rather like a latecomer to the dance and couldn't carry his burden. Durancos and I had more history, and we should have done more. But we didn't. That's just the start of it. There's more. But maybe it's time for that to change, too.

There is a photo of Clarence King that looks exactly like Tee Trundler, so exact, it's uncanny.

Deep Creek

The hairy boy band has disbanded, and we live in different places: Sean in Salt Lake, Don in southwestern Colorado, me in southern Utah. We try to get together in Good Water to play horseshoes and reminisce about old times. A reunion tour is unlikely.

I have no idea what happened to the maps in Tee's map room, the paper and pin records of many great days. Of Lady Teemore, the news is dismal; she dies of natural causes within seven years.

Those of us who have chosen to carry on have our own maps now, and they outline trips and times with our better halves, and our children. Jennifer, Larissa and Christy deserve some sort of reward, surely, because they saw something in us to make it worth most of the trouble, but don't actually ask them. They'd give another answer, surely.

RED STONE HEART

When we lived in Wyoming, the best cross-country skiing was in Utah, just over the border, in the East End of the Uintas, at Deep Creek, which owing the scarceness of other skiers, and the general absence of rare but always-welcome trail-packers (snow machiners), we nearly always had strictly to ourselves. We skied there dozens of times, Jennifer and I, and Chris. We took him everywhere. At first Chris was carried in the tortuous backpack, but singing on the downhills or napping, slopped over to the side. Next, I pulled him in a little red sled. Then, it was the sled and the threat of skis. Then it was skis and the threat of going even further. His big deal was always to pack a little hill and practice going up and down it. We reached a kind of compromise. Ski a bit. Then pack a hill and yo-yo a bit more.

When Katie or Jacque were willing to babysit, we left him with them, and Deep Creek was ours. Cold as it was, too, it was seldom the place for rapt contemplation. Even in midday, the winter temperatures urged movement not sitting. This allowed it to be broken down to its simplest form: kick and glide through the frozen land, on the white meadows and flats beneath the dark timbered slopes and ridges.

When we stayed at Red Canyon Lodge, we could ski across Green Lake at night, which was like skiing it in the day, but darker. The winds kept the snow shallow and fast, and the creaking ice and occasional bubble-up sounded like whale song.

Today, some years later, Young Christopher views cross-country skiing as a cruel form of torture, greatly preferring riding lifts and skiing fast (faster than his parents). And then he decides he doesn't want to ski at all.

But skiing helps keep Jennifer and me together.

Free of heel for thirty years, at fifty we clamp down and haven't looked back. Thanks for asking.

Jennifer continues to hone her skills and remains a strong and graceful skier, specializing in rhythmic parallels of the giant slalom type. She's both aggressive and crafty. There are very few women still skiing at her age, and she can easily leave them behind in the crud. Nor can I leave her alone in the lodge. If I go to the powder room, some lonesome dude will start chatting her up.

Jennifer grew up in Logan and learned to ski at an early age at Beaver Mountain. When we first started dating, Still-Young Kevin couldn't believe that he had found someone who was smart as hell, very good looking, and graceful on the two planks. To be frank, for the nearly thirty years we've called each other wax and iron, we've skied together every weekend in season in various ways and means. It's kept us together during the lean white ribbons and the monster dumps, the January thaw and the slush of April, on corduroy and crud, in hardpack and hoar, off *piste* and through the trees, with heels free and fixed.

And here's to it: the ever-changing, the places with spruce and fir and aspen, and the open spaces, blue-shadowed and frosty with poofder and rime, and a better half to do it with.

And, you know, if it's too much Denali, you can always go to the condo or lodge.

Thank goodness Sister Dona found an activity for Young Kevin.

RED STONE HEART

Once I find a place I like, I enjoy going back to it repeatedly. Is it possible to go back too many times? Is it possible to wear it out? Does the trail, which is never the same, become too much the same?

In this connection, bagging a peak has a certain advantage: once it's been done, one seldom even considers a return.

My journey has had a few such places that I've really gotten to know. Big Cottonwood, S & M, Big Sandy, Good Water, Deep Creek, Brian Head. Once you shut a door, though, you can't go back.

Now, I've been to London, seen Seven Wonders, but I've kept pretty much to my home ground, a restless serial adventurist. Maybe it's a failure of imagination. Maybe there was just plenty enough to go around.

Here's hoping you find your places, too, and good people to find them with. Why not begin now?

Kevin, Lovenia 2007